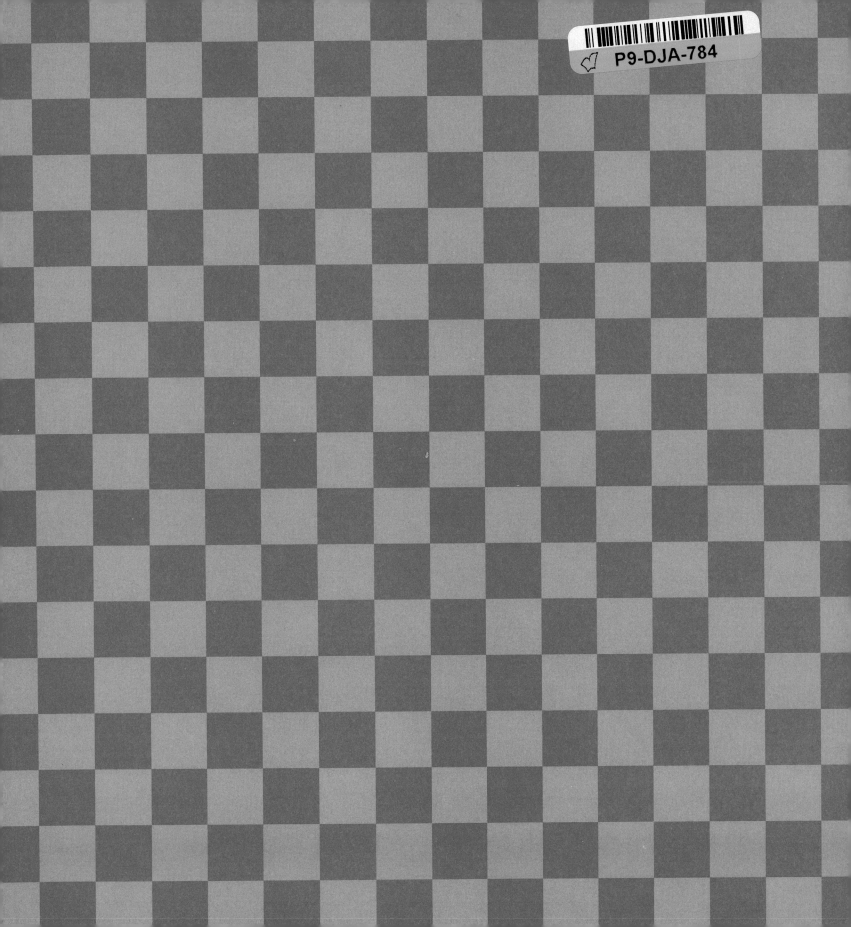

Better Homes and Gardens®

halloween
101 frightfully fun ideas

Better Homes and Gardens® Books
Des Moines, Iowa

Better Homes and Gardens® Books
An imprint of Meredith® Books

Halloween: 101 Frightfully Fun Ideas
Editor: Carol Field Dahlstrom
Technical Editor: Susan M. Banker
Graphic Designer: Angela Haupert Hoogensen
Copy Chief: Catherine Hamrick
Copy and Production Editor: Terri Fredrickson
Book Production Managers: Pam Kvitne,
    Marjorie J. Schenkelberg
Contributing Copy Editor: Carol Boker
Contributing Proofreaders: Becky Danley,
    Diane Doro, Mary Duerson, Colleen Johnson,
    Sheila Mauck, Lisa Stone
Photographers: Andy Lyons Cameraworks,
    Hopkins Associates, Peter Krumhardt, Scott Little
Technical Illustrator: Chris Neubauer Graphics, Inc.
Electronic Production Coordinator: Paula Forest
Editorial and Design Assistants: Judy Bailey,
    Mary Lee Gavin, Karen Schirm

Meredith® Books
Editor in Chief: James D. Blume
Design Director: Matt Strelecki
Managing Editor: Gregory H. Kayko

Director, Retail Sales and Marketing: Terry Unsworth
Director, Sales, Special Markets: Rita McMullen
Director, Sales, Premiums: Michael A. Peterson
Director, Sales, Retail: Tom Wierzbicki
Director, Sales, Home & Garden Centers: Ray Wolf
Director, Book Marketing: Brad Elmitt
Director, Operations: George A. Susral
Director, Production: Douglas M. Johnston

Vice President, General Manager: Jamie L. Martin

Better Homes and Gardens® Magazine
Editor in Chief: Jean LemMon
Executive Food Editor: Nancy Byal

Meredith Publishing Group
President, Publishing Group: Christopher M. Little
Vice President, Consumer Marketing & Interactive
    Media: Hal Oringer

Meredith Corporation
Chairman and Chief Executive Officer: William T. Kerr

Chairman of the Executive Committee: E. T. Meredith III

All of us at Better Homes and Gardens® Books are dedicated to providing you with information and ideas to create beautiful and useful projects. We welcome your comments and suggestions. Write to us at: Better Homes and Gardens Books, Crafts Editorial Department, 1716 Locust St., Des Moines, IA 50309-3023.

If you would like to purchase any of our books, check wherever quality books are sold. Visit our website at bhg.com or bhgbooks.com.

Designers: Susan M. Banker, Donna Chesnut, Carol
    Field Dahlstrom, Phyllis Dobbs, Phyllis Dunstan,
    Margaret Sindelar, Barb Smith, Alice Wetzel

Cover Photograph: Andy Lyons Cameraworks

Photographers: Andy Lyons Cameraworks, Hopkins
    Associates, Peter Krumhardt, Scott Little

Photo Styling Assistant: Donna Chesnut

Permission to photocopy patterns and create projects for individual use and sale is granted from Better Homes and Gardens® Books.

Our seal assures you that every recipe in *Halloween: 101 Frightfully Fun Ideas* has been tested in the Better Homes and Gardens® Test Kitchen. This means that each recipe is practical and reliable, and meets our high standards of taste appeal. We guarantee your satisfaction with this book for as long as you own it.

halloween

Get ready for tricks and treats, fun and fright—it's Halloween! What better time to plan a party, trim the haunted halls, and enjoy delicious treats than on the eeriest, silliest, spookiest night of the year.

Halloween is a wonderful time to get together with special friends and family members. Whether for a merrymaking trick-or-treat outing or a masquerade party at home, we'll help you celebrate in style.

Come along as we share Halloween ideas to transform your home into a haunted house or simply add a festive touch here and there. From unforgettable pumpkins to centerpieces and lighting ideas, your house will be the talk of the neighborhood.

If a party is in the plans, you'll enjoy recipes for can't-resist snack mixes, tempting drink concoctions, sandwiches any monster will love, and sweets so yummy you'll wish Halloween came every month. We'll even show you some great invitations you can make and decorations to make party goers giggle.

To encourage imaginations to soar, there are oh-so-clever costume ideas. No matter if you have just minutes or an entire weekend to devote, you'll find a costume that will be a treat to wear.

We hope you enjoy all of the creative ideas in this book and that they inspire you to put a little more spirit in the holiday. Happy Halloween!

Carol Field Dahlstrom

contents

just

All dressed up
and ready to glow

pumpkins

the crow's hideout

Ready for Halloween mischief, these artificial birds perched on the pumpkin-turned-birdhouse retreat appear to be real. Great for a centerpiece or last-minute trick-or-treat greeter, this quick pumpkin idea offers something to crow about.

supplies
- Pumpkin
- Knife, drill and large drill bit, or small, round cookie cutter
- 5-inch-long piece of ¼-inch dowel
- Pencil sharpener
- Paintbrush
- Acrylic paints in black and white
- 3 artificial crows
- Scissors; ruler
- White paper
- Tracing paper
- Round pencil
- Black marker
- Medium-gauge wire; nail
- Raffia or straw

what to do

1 Cut a round circle in the pumpkin on the lower half as shown, *opposite*. You can use a knife, a drill and bit, or a small, round cookie cutter.

2 Sharpen one end of the dowel in a pencil sharpener. Paint the dowel black and let it dry. Add white dots by dipping the handle end of a paintbrush into paint and dotting onto the dowel. Let dry. Insert the sharp end of the dowel just below the cutout. Attach a crow to the perch. Firmly press the wire feet of the remaining crows into the pumpkin top where desired.

3 To make a "Happy Halloween" sign, cut a 5×1⅝-inch piece from white paper. Trace the lettering, *below,* onto tracing paper. Place the traced pattern under white paper and hold up to a window for light. Use a black marker to copy the lettering. Outline the paper edges with marker. Poke two small holes in the top of the sign as shown, *opposite.* Cut a 5-inch length of wire. Curl it by wrapping around a pencil. Push the ends of the wire into the holes in the sign and twist to secure. Insert the nail into the pumpkin to hang the sign. Fill the drilled hole with raffia or straw.

SIGN PATTERN

pumpkin pizzazz

Small pumpkins get big applause with simple-to-do techniques. The pumpkin, opposite, has Halloween words spelled out in alphabet macaroni and is accented with metallic paints.

The star version, below, becomes a dazzling delight covered with glistening stars of all colors.

spell-cast pumpkin

supplies
Pumpkin
Alphabet macaroni
Paintbrush
Glossy decoupage medium
Acrylic metallic paints in copper, green, purple, gold, or other desired colors
Pencil with round-tip eraser

what to do
1 Decide what words or phrases to add to the pumpkin. Find the letters in the alphabet macaroni to spell out your selection. Use the paintbrush to add a ⅛-inch-thick line of decoupage medium on the pumpkin where you want to add the macaroni. Place the macaroni letters on the decoupage medium, spelling out the Halloween words or phrases of choice. Continue adding selections until you like how it looks. Let the decoupage medium dry.

2 To add color to the macaroni letters, paint the top surfaces only, using very little metallic paint. Use only one color on the entire word or phrase so it stands out as a unit. Let the paint dry.

3 To add dots between the words, dip the eraser end of the pencil into copper paint. Carefully dot the paint onto the surface of the pumpkin where desired. Let the paint dry.

star-struck pumpkin

supplies
Star-shaped gems
Pumpkin
Silicone adhesive

what to do
1 Place all of the stars right side up so the colors can be seen. Decide how closely you want the stars placed.

2 Put a dab of silicone adhesive on the back of each star and press into place on the pumpkin. Let the glue dry.

This friendly ghost, peeking from his pumpkin home, is fun to make from lightweight clay. With a few bright details, this clever pumpkin becomes the center of attention at your Halloween party.

spooky surprise

supplies

- **Small pumpkin**
- **Knife**
- **Spoon**
- **Four 8-inch-long pieces of ¼-inch dowel**
- **Pencil sharpener**
- **Acrylic paints in lime green and purple**
- **Paintbrush**
- **White Crayola® Model Magic® clay**
- **2 small black beads**
- **1 large black bead**
- **Toothpicks**
- **Shredded colored paper**

what to do

1 Cut the pumpkin in half horizontally, keeping the cut line as smooth as possible. Clean out the inside by scraping it with a spoon.

2 Sharpen both ends of the dowels in a pencil sharpener, for easy insertion into the pumpkin. Paint two dowel pieces lime green and the remaining two purple. Let the paint dry. Add dots on each dowel by dipping the handle end of the paintbrush into paint and dotting onto the dowel surfaces. Let the paint dry. Paint the pumpkin stem purple. Let dry. Add green dots. Let dry. Insert the dowels into the bottom half of the pumpkin, then place the pumpkin top on by firmly pressing it onto the dowels.

3 To create the ghost, take a portion of clay suitable for the size of your pumpkin. Knead the clay until it is smooth. Shape the clay into an oblong smooth piece. Gently twist the top portion to create a ghostly head. Shape arms from small pieces of dough. Position the arms onto the ghost's body and press into place. Form the bottom of the ghost to fit inside the pumpkin.

4 Use the photograph, *below,* as a guide to make the eyes and mouth. Press the black beads into the face using a toothpick. Press toothpicks into the bottom of the pumpkin. Position the ghost over the toothpicks and press into place.

5 Add shredded paper around the pumpkin.

silver swirl pumpkin

Long after the jack-o'-lantern candles are blown out, this silver-laden pumpkin will shine on. Use it as a beautiful centerpiece or front porch decoration all autumn long perched on a bed of leaves or sitting all by itself. When the time comes to toss out the pumpkin, the solder swirls can be pulled out and saved to use year after year.

supplies
Lead-free solder in desired thicknesses
Wire cutter
Needle-nose pliers
Ice pick
Pumpkin

what to do

1 Using the wire cutter, cut 2- to 8-inch lengths from the solder. Approximately 50 pieces will be needed to trim a medium-size pumpkin like the one shown, *opposite.*

2 Using the photographs, *opposite* and *right,* as guides, twist the solder lengths into desired shapes. Use a needle-nose pliers to start bending the end of the solder into a small loop. You can bend the solder lengths into coils, S-shapes, zigzags, or whatever you wish. Leave an inch at the end of the solder to bend perpendicular to the shape. This end of the solder will poke into the pumpkin to hold the solder shape in place.

3 Use an ice pick to poke holes in the pumpkin, approximately 3 to 5 inches apart. Insert the bent ends of the solder shapes into the holes to secure.

4 To add a solder shape to the pumpkin stem, first poke a hole in the stem using an ice pick. Shape a length of wire as desired, leaving 1 inch at an end to insert into the stem. Push the solder into the pumpkin stem.

metal magic

Add a stylish twist to make any pumpkin stand out from the rest. Cut from copper foil, the leaves poke easily into a pumpkin top, opposite. The coordinating pair, left and below, can be made in minutes using eyelets and grommets.

copper-leafed pumpkin

supplies
Tracing paper
Pencil
Old scissors
36-gauge copper tooling foil
Dish towel
Pointed skewer
20-gauge copper wire
Knife
Pumpkin

what to do
1 Trace the leaf patterns, *right,* onto tracing paper. Cut out shapes. Draw around leaf shapes on copper tooling foil. Cut out leaf shapes.

2 To make the leaf veins, first place the leaves on a dish towel. Using the pattern as a guide, make vein impressions using a skewer.

3 Cut four 14-inch lengths of wire. Wrap the wire lengths around the skewer and remove. Pull apart as desired to make curlicues.

4 Cut two small slits, each about 1 inch long, next to the pumpkin stem. Insert one tip of each leaf into a slit. Shape leaves as desired.

5 Twist the ends of the wire spirals together and press into the pumpkin near where the leaves are inserted.

rings pumpkin

supplies
Pumpkin
Gold grommets
Spoon, if needed
Gold and copper eyelets

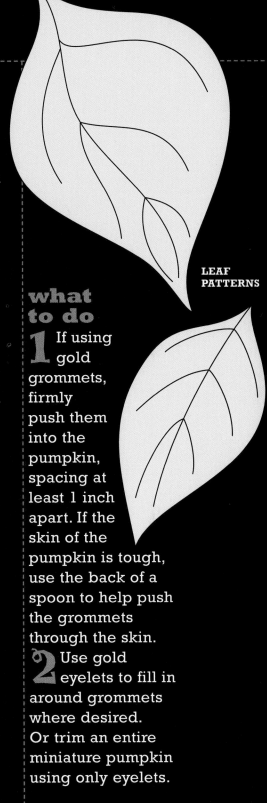

LEAF PATTERNS

what to do
1 If using gold grommets, firmly push them into the pumpkin, spacing at least 1 inch apart. If the skin of the pumpkin is tough, use the back of a spoon to help push the grommets through the skin.

2 Use gold eyelets to fill in around grommets where desired. Or trim an entire miniature pumpkin using only eyelets.

fallen leaves pumpkin

The colors of autumn are vividly enhanced by painting gathered leaves with bright metallic paints. A white pumpkin creates an unexpected, ghostlike backdrop for these favorite symbols of the fall season.

supplies
Dry leaves
Newspapers
Acrylic metallic paints in lime green, magenta, blue, and purple
Paintbrush
White pumpkin
Decoupage medium

what to do

1 Gather leaves in desired sizes and shapes. Make sure the leaves are dry but not brittle. Green leaves may curl and will not accept paint well.

2 Cover your work surface with newspapers. Paint the front sides of the leaves using metallic paints. Let the paint dry. Apply a second coat if needed. Let the paint dry. Turn the leaves over and paint the back, using the same color. Let the paint dry.

3 Paint the stem of the pumpkin using a desired color of metallic paint. Let the paint dry.

4 To attach the leaves to the top and sides of the pumpkin, coat the back of each leaf with decoupage medium. The leaves will not stay flat to the pumpkin, but will curl a bit. Press a leaf onto the pumpkin and paint over the front of the leaf with a coat of decoupage medium. Continue adding leaves in this manner until the desired look is achieved. Let it dry.

pretty patterned pumpkins

Using brushstrokes of metallic paint adds a contemporary touch to this beauty from the pumpkin patch. The details complementing the checkerboard pattern are made with easy-to-do dots and scribbles from a permanent marking pen.

Colorful plastic-coated wires seem to grow on the miniature pumpkin. Holes poked in the pumpkin anchor the vertical wires and separate wires twist around the stem.

check-it-out pumpkin

supplies
Acrylic metallic paints in teal and purple
1-inch flat paintbrush
Pumpkin
Metallic gold permanent marking pen
Pencil with round-tip eraser

what to do
1 Paint a teal checkerboard design on the pumpkin. To begin, start with the center of the pumpkin. Paint 1-inch squares around the center of the pumpkin. Continue making 1-inch checks over the entire pumpkin, alternating the positions as shown, *opposite*. Let the paint dry.

2 To add squiggles, draw them on top of the painted checkerboard as desired. Let it dry.

3 To add dots between the painted checks, dip the eraser end of a pencil into purple paint. Carefully dot on the surface where desired. Let the paint dry.

wire-wrapped pumpkin

supplies
Ice pick
Miniature pumpkin
Plastic-coated wire in desired colors
Old scissors

what to do
1 Using an ice pick, poke tiny holes at the top of each pumpkin crevice around the stem. Repeat on the bottom of the pumpkin.

2 Cut lengths of wire to reach from a top hole to a bottom hole, adding 2 inches. Bend over 1 inch at the end of a wire length. Push the short folded-over end into a hole at the top of the pumpkin. Gently pull the wire down the crevice of the pumpkin and firmly push the remaining wire end into the hole at the bottom. Repeat for each set of holes.

3 Cut a 3-inch piece of each color of wire. Twist together at one end. Wrap around stem as desired.

This pair of pumpkins makes quite a team when the top pumpkin nests on top of the base. Their playful expressions make them appear as if they're sharing the latest Halloween gags. Our Golden Girl, right, is all dressed up with curly locks and a pretty bow.

kooky characters

joking, jesting buddies

supplies
Knife
Large, round pumpkin
Large, tall pumpkin
Spoon
Fine permanent marking pen
Two votive candles
Match

what to do
1 Cut the top off each pumpkin and scoop out the insides using a spoon. Place the tall pumpkin on top of the round pumpkin. If necessary, enlarge the hole in the top of the round pumpkin so the tall one sits as shown.

2 Looking at the photograph, *opposite,* as a guide, draw faces on the pumpkins so that they look as if they're talking to each other. Cut out face shapes using a knife.

3 Place a candle in the round jack-o'-lantern and light. Position the tall pumpkin atop the round one. Place a candle in the tall jack-o'-lantern and light. Put on the lid. Be sure not to leave a burning candle unattended.

golden girl

supplies
Small, round pumpkin
Black eyelets
Black chenille stems
Round pencil, dowel, or skewer
Ice pick
Scissors
12-inch pieces of ribbon

what to do
1 Push an eyelet into the center of the pumpkin for the nose. Using the photograph, *right,* as a guide, make two triangular eyes and a smile using eyelets.

2 To make the hair, tightly wrap each chenille stem around a pencil, dowel, or skewer, and remove. Use an ice pick to make holes in the top of the

pumpkin where you want to add hair. Push the ends of the chenille stems into the holes. For bangs, cut chenille stems in half.

3 Tie two or three ribbons to the stem and allow to trail through the hair.

23

web-laden pumpkin

When the light falls upon this pumpkin, the glitter paint and faceted gems will sparkle with vibrant color. The web effect is easy to achieve by simply outlining the pumpkin crevices with a paint pen.

supplies
Pumpkin
Metallic paint pens in purple and gold
Gems in oval and rectangular shapes
Small metallic beads to match gems

what to do

1 To draw the spider web, use metallic purple paint pen. Start by following the vertical crevices in the pumpkin. Use the photographs, *opposite* and *right,* as guides, making the lines different lengths. When all of the vertical lines are painted, draw the horizontal lines, making them slightly scalloped and about 1 inch apart. Let the paint pen dry.

2 Decide where to add spiders. Place a small amount of metallic gold paint pen on the back of the gem for body. Use an oval gem for a large spider or a rectangular gem for a small spider. Place onto the pumpkin. If making a large spider, use a rectangular gem for the head. Place paint pen on the back of the gem and place it above the oval body. Outline the spiders using metallic gold paint pen. Press two bead eyes to the top of the head. Add paint pen legs and let dry.

3 Paint the stem of the pumpkin using metallic gold paint pen. Let the paint pen dry.

Master the trick to this pumpkin using cookie cutters to make the star shapes. The larger stars are carved through the entire pumpkin skin and flesh, while the small ones leave a thin layer of pumpkin flesh for the light to glow through.

glowing star pumpkin

supplies
Knife; spoon
Pumpkin
Star cookie
  cutters in
  desired sizes
Paring knife
Tracing paper
Metallic gold
  permanent
  marking pen
Toothpick
Candle
Match

what to do

1 Cut the top third off the pumpkin. Clean out the insides using a spoon.

2 Press a large cookie cutter into the pumpkin where you want the large stars cut out. Remove the cookie cutter and use a paring knife to carefully cut out the shapes. (If you do not have star cookie cutters, trace the patterns, *right*. Cut out patterns and trace star shapes on the pumpkin using gold marker. Use a knife to cut shapes from pumpkin.)

3 For the small stars, press the small star cookie cutter into the skin of the pumpkin, being careful not to pierce through the entire skin. Use a paring knife to remove the outer layer of skin, leaving a thin lining for the light to shine through.

4 Outline the star shapes with metallic gold marker. Use the marker to add squiggles between the star shapes, if desired.

5 Poke a toothpick into the bottom of one of the medium-size stars removed from the pumpkin. Color in the star shape using metallic gold marker. Color the raised areas of the stem using marker.

6 Poke a hole in the top of the stem. Insert the toothpick with the star on the end.

7 Place a candle inside the pumpkin, light the wick, and place the lid on the pumpkin. (Never leave a burning candle unattended.)

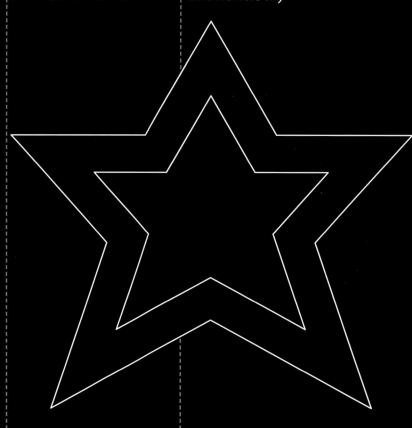

STAR PATTERNS

jester jack-o'-lantern

Any pumpkin, carved or fresh from the pumpkin patch, will look grand sitting upon this whimsical garden post. Trimmed with star-shape wood cutouts and beads on colored wires, the brightly painted post stands 4 feet tall.

supplies

Pumpkin; spoon
Knife
Wood garden post
Saw; sandpaper
11×11-inch piece of ¾-inch-thick pine
Flower-shape wood clock face or 9-inch-square piece of ¾-inch-thick pine
Tack cloth
Acrylic paints in orange, black, yellow, purple, green, and white
Paintbrush; pencil
Tracing paper
Four 3-inch wood stars; five 1¾-inch wood stars
Twenty ¾-inch wood stars
Wood finial
Wood glue
Drill and drill bit
Six 2-inch-long wood screws with flat heads
Screwdriver
Assorted beads
Colored wire
Ice pick; toothpick
Candle; match

what to do

1 Cut the top off the pumpkin in a zigzag pattern. Clean out the insides with a spoon. Carve a face on the pumpkin. Set it aside.

2 If desired, cut off the bottom of the garden post so it measures approximately 4 feet high. Sand any rough spots on the garden post, clock face, or remaining pine pieces. Remove any dust using a tack cloth.

3 Using the photograph, *right,* for ideas, paint the garden post. You can paint solid areas, checks, stripes, dots, or whatever you wish. To make the triangular shapes at the top of the

continued on page 31

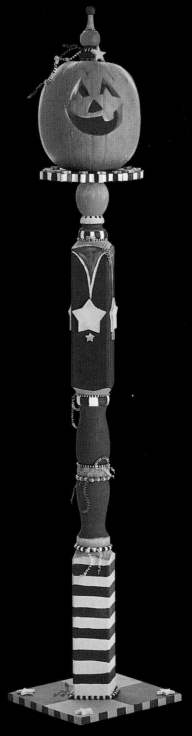

STAND TOP PATTERN

FOLD

large stars, paint them green with a little yellow mixed in. Let the paint dry. Outline the lower edges of the triangles with yellow. For all other green painted areas, highlight with yellow while the green paint is wet. For the yellow areas, you can add touches of orange while the yellow paint is wet. When painting a black-and-white checked pattern, paint the entire area white first. When dry, add the black checks.

4 For the base, divide the top into four equal sections, drawing in the lines with a pencil. Paint two opposite corners orange and the remaining two black. Let the paint dry. Paint the edges with black and orange, creating a checked pattern. Let the paint dry.

5 For the wood piece that sits on the top of the post, use the wood clock face. If you prefer to cut a top piece from pine, trace the pattern, *opposite.* Cut out the pattern and trace around it on pine. Use a band saw to cut out the shape. Sand the edges if necessary. Paint the top solid purple and the edge with a black-and-white checked design. Let the paint dry. Add orange and green dots to the top edge, if desired. Let dry.

6 Paint the large and medium stars yellow. Dry-brush the edges using orange. Let the paint dry. Paint twelve of the small stars orange and the remaining stars yellow. Add yellow to the edges of the orange stars and orange to the edges of the yellow stars. Let dry.

7 Paint the finial as desired, using the photograph, *page 28,* for ideas. Let the paint dry.

8 Glue the large stars on the garden post as shown. Add a small star below each large one. Glue a medium star in each corner of the base piece. Glue small stars around the edge of the top piece, alternating orange and yellow stars. Let dry.

9 Drill a hole through the center of the round top piece. Drill a hole in the center of the top and bottom of the post. Drill a hole through the center of the base piece. Use screws to secure the base and top pieces to the post.

10 Tighten to secure. Thread desired beads onto wires. Put enough beads on to wrap around post where you want to add the beaded wires. Tie the wires in place. To curl the wire ends, wrap tightly around an ice pick.

11 Remove top from the pumpkin. Use an ice pick to poke a hole 1 inch deep in the stem of the pumpkin. Glue a toothpick in the hole. Place painted finial on toothpick. Add beaded wires and a wooden star to the topper.

12 Carefully place the pumpkin on stand, making sure it is balanced. Place a candle in the pumpkin and light it. Place on the lid. Be sure to never leave a burning candle unattended.

tricks

Goodies you'll want to concoct

'n' treats

monster mixes

A bewitching blend of sweet surprises will satisfy anyone's cravings for a snack. The painted jars are just right to hold a generous portion, and can serve as votive candleholders once the handles are removed. The instructions and mix recipe are on page 37. For more snack mixes and fun containers, turn the page.

PAINTED TOTE TRIO
AND CREEPY CANDY MIX

**OOKY 'N' SPOOKY TREAT CUPS
AND HONEY 'N' SPICE POPCORN**

**GHOULISH GOODY
JAR AND
GREMLIN GORP**

**BODY
BITS**

Glass paints in
   black, green,
   yellow, orange,
   purple, and white
Paintbrush;
   pencil with
   round-tip eraser
Chenille stems in
   black, orange,
   purple, and
   yellow

what to do

1 Wash and dry
   each jar or
glass. Avoid
touching the areas
to be painted.

2 Trace the
   desired
patterns, *page 38,*
onto tracing
paper. Cut out the
patterns slightly
beyond the drawn

Let the paint dry.
Use the photographs
on *pages 34–35* to
paint on the details.
If paints are layered,
be sure to let the
paint dry between
coats. To add small
dots, dip the handle
end of a paintbrush
into paint and dot
onto the surface.
For the larger dots,
use the eraser end
of a pencil.

4 To make a
   handle, use two
contrasting chenille
stems. Align ends
and twist 1 inch
from the ends.
Bring long ends
around jar top, one
in front and one in
back. Continue

supplies
1 8-ounce bag
   candy-coated,
   peanut butter-
   flavor pieces
1 cup candy corn
1 10½-ounce bag
   miniature
   marshmallows

what to do
1 Toss the
   ingredients
together in a
mixing bowl.
Makes about 7 cups.

ooky 'n'
spooky
treat cups

supplies
**Clear plastic
   punch cups**

Pencil; scissors
Tape
Glass paints in
   black, green,
   yellow, and white
Paintbrush
Flat glass marbles
   in iridescent
   black and frosted
   clear or pale green
Silicone glue

what to do

1 Wash and dry
   the cups. Avoid
touching the areas
to be painted.

2 If painting the
   cat, trace the
pattern onto
tracing paper. Cut
out slightly beyond
the drawn lines.

continued on page 38

**PAINTED TOTE TRIO
CAT PATTERN**

**PAINTED TOTE TRIO
SWIRL PATTERN**

**PAINTED TOTE TRIO
PUMPKIN PATTERN**

monster mixes
continued

Tape the pattern to the inside of the jar where you wish to paint the design. Place it low on the cup so the weight of the eyes does not tip the cup.

3 To make the cat cup, paint the cat black. Let the paint dry. Use the photograph on *page 36* to paint on the nose, mouth, and whisker details. To paint the marble eyes, mix a drop of green and yellow. Paint long ovals on the front sides of two frosted marbles. Let the paint dry. Paint smaller black ovals inside of the green ones. Let the paint dry. Glue the eyes in place and let dry.

4 To make the spider, glue two iridescent black marbles on the cup. Place them low enough so the cup does not tip. Let the glue dry. Paint on black legs. Let the paint dry.

honey 'n' spice popcorn

supplies
**10 cups popped
  corn (about
  $1/2$ cup unpopped)
1 cup peanuts
$1/4$ cup honey
3 tablespoons
  margarine
$1/4$ teaspoon
  pumpkin pie
  spice**

what to do
1 Place popped corn and peanuts in a large roasting pan. In a small saucepan combine honey, margarine, and pumpkin pie spice. Heat and stir till margarine melts. Pour over popcorn and nuts, tossing to coat.

2 Bake in a 300° oven for 30 minutes, stirring about every 10 minutes. Transfer to a baking sheet; cool. Makes about 10 cups.

ghoulish goody jar

supplies
Jar with lip
Glass paints in black, green, yellow, orange, and white
Paintbrushes
Pencil with round-tip eraser
Black and white chenille stems

what to do
1 Wash and dry the jar. Avoid touching the areas to be painted. Paint black checks around the jar as shown on *page 36*, creating as many rows as the jar will allow. To create a row of lime green dots around the jar top, mix together a small amount of yellow and green paints. Dip the handle end of a paintbrush into the paint and dot on the surface, just below the lip. Let dry.

2 Paint orange dots where the checks meet, using the eraser end of a pencil. Let dry.

3 Add a white dot to the center of each check and a lime green dot to the center of each orange dot. Let dry.

4 For handle, align the ends of the chenille stems and twist to secure 1 inch from the ends. Bring the long ends around the jar top, one in front and one in back. Continue twisting the chenille stems together, keeping tight to hold the jar. Shape the handle and twist all ends together to secure.

gremlin gorp

supplies
1 6-ounce bag dried apricots, snipped, for dried skin (1 cup)
2 4½-ounce boxes of bite-size round crackers for witches' warts
1 6-ounce bag dried cranberries or cherries for dried drops of dragons' blood (1⅔ cups)
1 12-ounce jar dry-roasted peanuts for dried lizards' eyes (2⅓ cups)

what to do
1 Toss together in mixing bowl. Store in airtight bag or container up to 3 days. Makes 9 cups.

body bits

supplies
2½ cups coarsely crushed blue corn chips
1 cup corn nuts
1 cup raisins
1 cup pretzel sticks
1 cup canned shoestring potatoes
1 cup cheese sticks
½ cup shelled pistachio nuts or peanuts
Marshmallow ghost

what to do
1 Put the crushed corn chips, corn nuts, raisins, pretzel sticks, shoestring potatoes, cheese sticks, and nuts in a serving bowl. Stir. Garnish with a marshmallow ghost. Makes 8 cups.

2 To store, place mix in a plastic bag or container; cover tightly. Store in a cool, dry place for up to 2 weeks.

CAULDRON
CUPCAKES

dressed-up cupcakes

Cupcakes are always yummy to eat—even when they look like witch's cauldrons. This brewing concoction, in the scooped-out center of a cupcake, is made from pudding, gel frosting, and tiny candies. For more Halloween cupcake ideas, turn to page 42.

supplies for all cupcakes

Baked cupcakes
Spoon
Chocolate and vanilla frosting
Vanilla pudding or yogurt
Gel tube frosting
Small candies
String licorice
Paste food coloring
Candy corn
Fruit leather
Gumdrops
Edible glitter

cauldron cupcakes

what to do

1 Remove paper from a purchased or baked cupcake. Turn cupcake upside down; trim bottom if necessary to make cupcake stand straight.

2 Using a spoon, scoop out center, leaving ½ inch around the edges and about 1 inch on the bottom. Spread chocolate frosting on the sides and top of each cupcake.

3 Spoon the vanilla pudding or yogurt into the center of the cupcake. Decorate it with green gel tube frosting. Sprinkle the small candies onto the fillings. Push the ends of the licorice into opposite sides of the cupcake to make a handle.

monster cupcakes

what to do

1 Tint half of a can of vanilla frosting with green paste food coloring. Frost the top of one cupcake with white frosting. Remove the paper from another cupcake. Frost the entire cupcake with green frosting. Press top of green frosted cupcake into the top of the other paper-lined cupcake, leaving a gap in front (see the photograph on *page 42*). Place candy corn in the gap to form teeth.

2 Decorate cupcakes with small candies, string licorice, fruit leather, and gel frosting to complete the monster's face.

continued on page 42

spider cupcakes

what to do

1 If desired, tint vanilla frosting with orange and yellow paste food coloring. Frost cupcakes with white, orange, or yellow frosting.

SPIDER CUPCAKES

Boo!

HAPPY HALLOWEEN

MESSAGE CUPCAKES

MONSTER CUPCAKES

42

2 Push eight 2-inch pieces of red and/or black string licorice into a large black, orange or yellow gumdrop, forming a spider and press into the top of each frosted cupcake. Sprinkle the cupcakes with edible glitter.

message cupcakes

supplies
Tracing paper
Round pencil
Scissors
Crafting foam in purple and orange
Black permanent marker
Thick white craft glue
5-inch pieces of wooden skewer
Chenille stems in purple, orange, and lime green
Paper punch

what to do
1 Trace the desired pattern, *right,* onto tracing paper. Cut out the pattern. Trace around the bat pattern on purple crafting foam or the jack-o'-lantern pattern on orange crafting foam. Cut out the shape.

2 Using the pattern for inspiration, draw in the features using permanent marker.

3 Glue a skewer to the back of the foam bat or pumpkin. Let the glue dry.

4 To add the green twist to the pumpkin, wrap a 4-inch piece of chenille stem around a pencil. Use a paper punch to add a hole near the stem in the pumpkin. Push one end of the chenille stem through the hole and twist to secure. To make the coils at the bottom, wrap an entire chenille stem around a pencil. Slip the skewer into the coil. Gently pull the coil apart until it covers 2 to 3 inches of the skewer. Push skewer into the center of the cupcake top.

MESSAGE CUPCAKES BAT PATTERN

MESSAGE CUPCAKES JACK-O'-LANTERN PATTERN

43

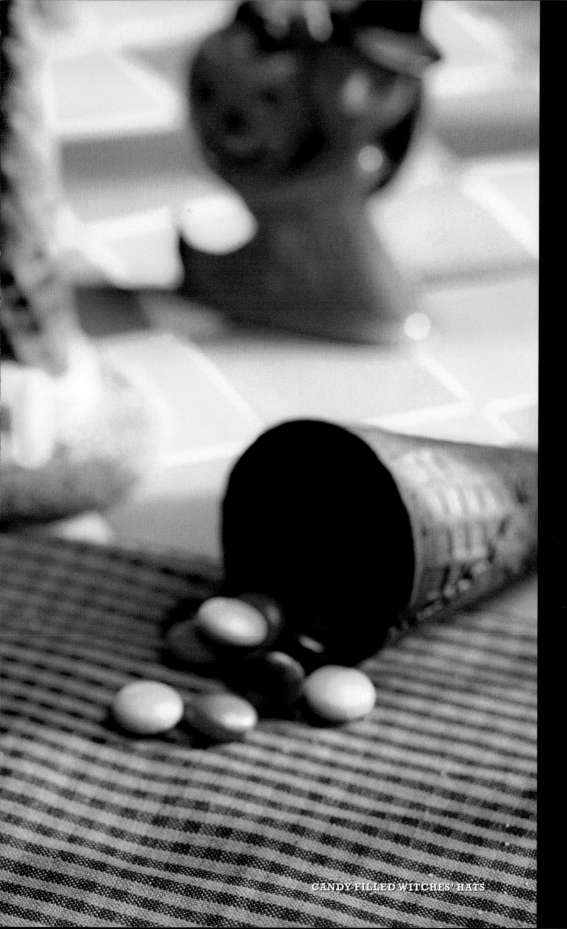

cookie treats

Hats off to these chocolate temptations made from ice cream cones and purchased cookies. Each cone is filled with candy treats before it is attached to the base, making for a sweet surprise. The instructions follow on page 47. For more cookie treat ideas, turn the page.

CANDY-FILLED WITCHES' HATS

45

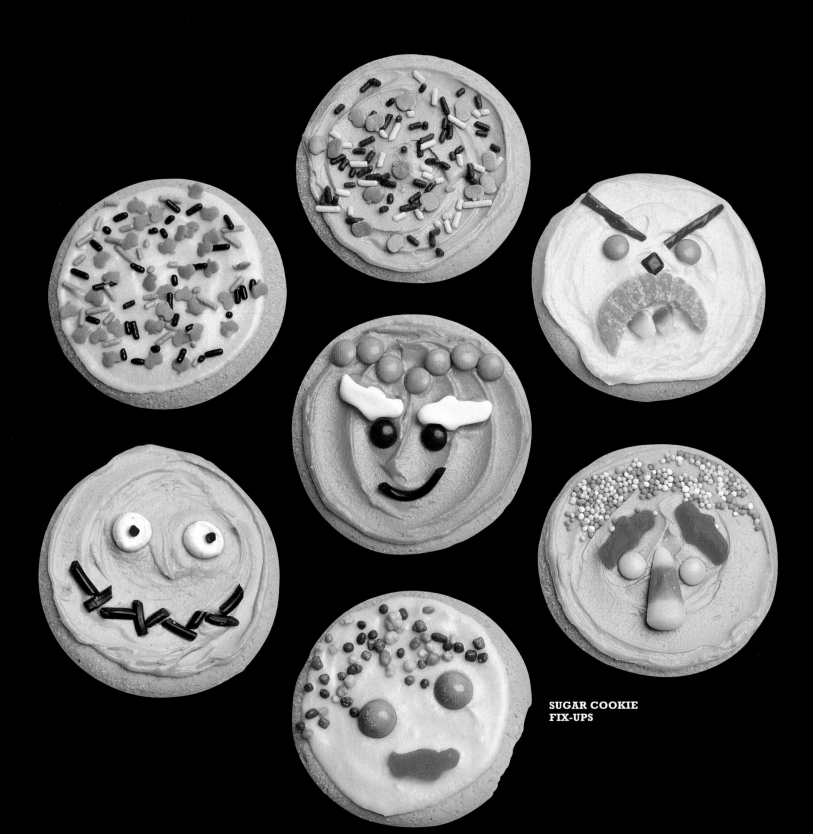

SUGAR COOKIE
FIX-UPS

46

candy-filled witches' hats

supplies

Self-sealing plastic bag
Can of chocolate frosting
Scissors
20 chocolate ice cream cones
Candy corn or assorted small candies
20 2- to 3-inch chocolate cookies
Waxed paper
Large green and yellow gumdrops

what to do

1 Fill a small self-sealing plastic bag with some chocolate frosting. Seal bag and cut a very small end off one corner of the bag and set aside. Invert cone and fill with about 2 tablespoons candy corn or small candies. Pipe some frosting from bag along bottom edge of cone. Press a cookie against frosting. Carefully invert right side up onto waxed paper-lined baking sheet.

2 Decorate outside of cone with small candies, using additional frosting as necessary. Refill frosting bag as needed. If desired, roll out large green and yellow gumdrops on a sugared surface until ⅛ inch thick. Cut into ¼-inch strips. Press green strips around brim of hat and cut smaller pieces from yellow strips to make a buckle; press onto hat. Makes 20 hats.

sugar cookie fix-ups

supplies

Orange, yellow, and green paste food color
1 16-ounce can vanilla frosting
Purchased plain sugar cookies
Tubes of colored decorating frosting (red, green, yellow)
Small candies

what to do

1 Add food coloring to purchased vanilla frosting, if desired, to make orange, yellow, and/or green frosting. Spread frosting on sugar cookies and decorate with tube frosting and small candies to make jack-o'-lanterns, ghosts, and monsters. See photos, *opposite* and *below*, for ideas.

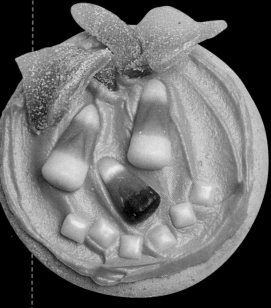

spooky house with ghosts and ghouls

Constructing this haunted house provides an opportunity for the kids to join in. You supply all the ingredients and watch them search their imaginations to make the edible house even more scary.

supplies

- 1 16-ounce can chocolate frosting
- Self-sealing plastic bags
- 16 honey graham cracker squares
- 4 chocolate graham cracker squares
- 1 clean 1-quart wax-coated paper milk carton
- Serrated knife
- 7 black licorice twists
- Small Halloween candy figures
- Small candies
- Green and yellow gel tube frosting
- Orange and yellow decorating sugars

what to do

1 Spoon some chocolate frosting into a plastic bag. Snip off one small corner. Fill bag with more frosting as needed. Pipe frosting from bag onto one side of a honey graham cracker square and press against one side of milk carton, even with bottom. Repeat with two more squares to cover one side. Repeat on remaining three sides. Cut two honey graham cracker squares diagonally from both bottom corners to center of top to form two triangle pieces for top of house; trim to fit. Pipe frosting on one side of both pieces and press into place on carton. Pipe frosting on one side of two chocolate graham cracker squares and press onto top of milk carton for roof. Pipe frosting onto corners of house. Press licorice in place.

2 To form a door, halve a chocolate graham cracker square and use frosting to attach one rectangle to the front bottom of house. Saw two honey graham cracker squares into two rectangles each. Pipe frosting around door and attach three of the honey graham rectangles to form an entryway. Cut small pieces of chocolate crackers for shutters. Pipe frosting onto one side of shutters and Halloween candy figures. Press onto sides of house for windows.

3 Decorate with candies, sugars, and gel frosting as desired.

witches' broomsticks

supplies

- 12 7-inch pretzel rods, 3/8 inch thick
- 6 pieces fruit-flavored licorice twists
- Cherry or apricot rolled fruit leather
- Black or red licorice string

what to do

1 Cut pretzel to 6-inch rods with a serrated knife. Quarter licorice twists lengthwise and then cut into 2-inch pieces. Place about 10 pieces around the cut end of a pretzel rod. Using an 8×1-inch piece of fruit leather, tightly wrap around the end of pretzel, securing the fruit licorice to the pretzel and pressing fruit leather in place. Tie with a small piece of licorice string. Snip ends of fruit licorice with scissors to form broom fringe. Makes 12.

jack -o'- lantern treat totes

Crepe paper isn't just for decorating ceilings anymore! Cut small squares from the roll and decoupage the pieces over a balloon to create a pumpkin shell that's all ready to carve. Fill with shredded paper pieces and wrapped goodies for little ones to enjoy. The instructions are on page 53.

jack-o'-lantern treat totes continued

supplies

Newspapers
Small balloons
Disposable foam
  plate
Crafts knife
Scissors
Orange crepe
  paper
Decoupage
  medium
Paintbrush
Small foam ball,
  such as
  Styrofoam
Colored papers in
  yellow, black,
  and purple
Thick white
  crafts glue
Small paper
  punch
Eyelets and
  eyelet tool
Plastic-coated
  colored wires in
  purple, black,
  white, orange,
  yellow, and
  green
Ice pick or skewer

what to do

1 Cover your work surface with newspapers. Blow up a balloon to be about the size of a baseball. Secure the end.

2 Cut a small X in the center of the foam plate using a crafts knife. From the top of the plate, pull the knot of the balloon to the back of the plate. This will help hold the balloon while you work.

3 Use scissors to cut several squares from the crepe paper roll. Cover the bottom two-thirds of the balloon with a coat of decoupage medium. Add crepe paper squares over this area, using decoupage medium to stick the pieces to the balloon. Continue adding more crepe paper squares until at least two layers cover the entire two-thirds of the balloon. Paint a coat of decoupage medium over the crepe paper. Let it dry.

4 Pop the balloon and remove it. Place a foam ball inside the crepe paper cup. Use a crafts knife to cut the desired face in one side.

5 Cut a circle or oval from the desired color of paper to fit inside the crepe paper cup, underneath the cut features. Glue the paper in place and let the glue dry.

6 Punch a hole on each side of the face, approximately 1 inch from the top. Insert an eyelet in the hole and secure it using the eyelet tool as directed on the tool package.

7 Braid or twist wires together to make a handle. Insert the wire ends through the eyelet holes. To finish the wire ends, wrap them around an ice pick or skewer.

53

surprise sacks

Get ready for candy riches with these bags trimmed in felt, buttons, and stitches! Find bags like these in a gift wrap department, or glue jute handles to brown paper lunch bags as an alternative. The patterns and instructions are on pages 56–57.

SCAREDY CAT

CAT PATTERN

OH PUMPKIN PUMPKIN PUMPKIN

PUMPKIN PATTERN

supplies
Tracing paper
Pencil
Scissors
Felt sheets in black, orange, green, and white
Sewing threads in orange and black
Sewing needle
1 orange and 4 blue beads
Glue stick
5x8-inch brown paper bags
Cotton embroidery floss in black, emerald green, and burnt orange
Assorted buttons in black, yellow, green, orange, and Halloween motifs

what to do
1 Trace the patterns, *opposite* and *right,* onto tracing paper and cut out. Using patterns, cut one of each pumpkin on orange felt, three pumpkin stems on green felt, one cat on black felt, and two ghosts on white felt. Cut out shapes.

2 Stitch two blue beads on each ghost and one orange bead to cat for eyes. Glue the felt shapes to paper bags using the photo on *pages 54–55* for placement.

3 Use three strands of floss to stitch straight stitches around the edges of the felt shapes. Stitch the pumpkin with emerald green floss, the cat with burnt orange floss, and the ghosts with emerald green floss.

4 With a pencil, lightly write "OH PUMPKIN PUMPKIN" on the pumpkin bag, "SCAREDY CAT" on the cat bag, and "CATCH ME" and "BOO" on the ghost bag. Draw curly vines to the center pumpkin stem. Using three strands of floss, stitch straight stitches to stitch "OH PUMPKIN PUMPKIN," "SCAREDY CAT," and vines with emerald green floss; "CATCH ME" with black floss; and "BOO" with burnt orange floss.

5 Stitch the buttons on the bags as desired.

GHOST PATTERN

CATCH ME

BOO

haunting

Scare them all night

decorations

Glittered wood masks add mysterious flair to this simple ring of grapevine. Cut the variety of mask shapes from plywood and drill holes at each side to attach them to the wreath. Wrap the entire ring with metallic star garland and this Halloween wreath gets the party off to an enchanting start.

supplies

Tracing paper
Pencil; scissors
1/4-inch-thick plywood
Jigsaw
Drill and 1/8-inch bit
Wood glue
Medium sandpaper
Acrylic paint in light green, orange, purple, and yellow
Paintbrush
Glitter in blue and multicolors
Wire
18-inch grapevine wreath
Multicolored star garland

what to do

1 Trace the patterns, *pages 62–63,* onto tracing paper and cut out. Trace around the shapes on the sheet of plywood.

2 Cut out the mask shapes using a jigsaw. To cut out the eyes, first drill a hole in each eye area on the mask. Use the hole as a starting area to cut out each eye shape. Drill side holes where indicated. For the masks with the nose pieces, cut two nose pieces. On the long edge, cut at a 45-degree angle. Glue these edges together and let dry. Sand any rough edges until smooth. Glue to the face piece. Let dry.

3 Paint the masks with acrylic paint using the photograph, *opposite,* for ideas. Paint masks one at a time and, while the paint is wet, sprinkle the desired color of glitter onto the paint. Let the paint dry. Shake off any excess glitter.

4 Cut ten 4-inch-long pieces of wire. Thread one piece through each side hole in the masks. Twist the ends to secure. Use these wires to attach the masks to the wreath.

5 Wrap the wreath with star garland as desired.

continued on page 62

NOSE
PIECE
PATTERN
(CUT 2)

BLUE
MASK
PATTERN

GOLD
MASK
PATTERN

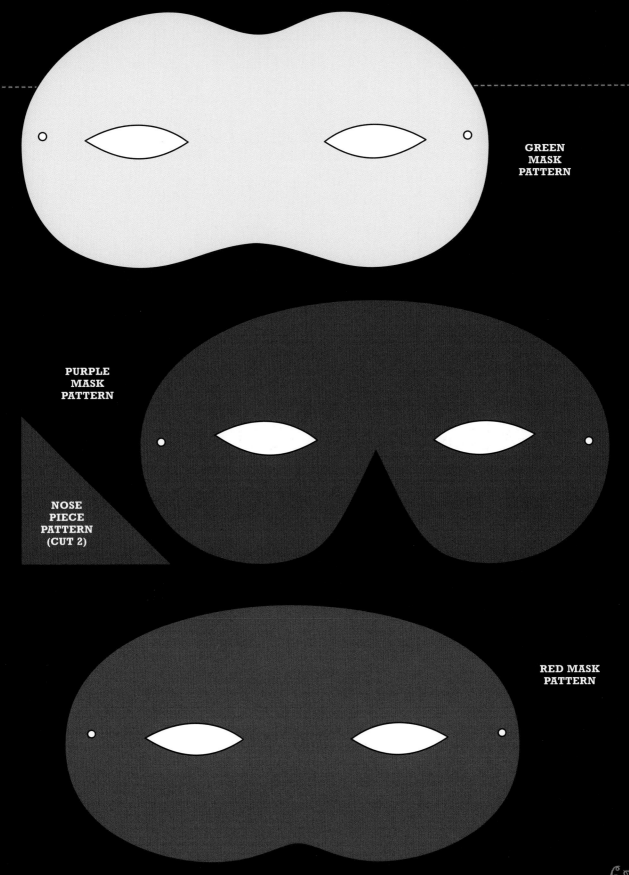

GREEN
MASK
PATTERN

PURPLE
MASK
PATTERN

NOSE
PIECE
PATTERN
(CUT 2)

RED MASK
PATTERN

63

Round glass ornaments transform quickly into a gathering of Halloween trims. Hung from fallen branches that are spray-painted purple, these ornaments celebrate the holiday with style. The instructions for all the ornaments begin on page 68.

halloween tree trims

JACK-O'-LANTERN ORNAMENT

HALLOWEEN SWIRL ORNAMENT

**POLKA-DOT
ORNAMENTS**

**STARRY NIGHT
ORNAMENT**

**SPIDER-'N'-WEB
ORNAMENT**

BOO-TO-YOU ORNAMENT

polka-dot ornaments

supplies

Round purple or
  green ornament
Newspapers; string
Glass paints in
  black, orange,
  yellow, purple,
  and green
Disposable foam
  plate
Pencil with
  round-tip eraser
Clear iridescent
  glitter, if desired
Toothpick or
  paintbrush
5 inches of lime
  green sequins on
  a string; thick
  white crafts glue
1/8- to 1/4-inch-wide
  ribbon

what to do

1 Wash and dry
  the ornament.
Avoid touching the
areas to be painted.

2 Cover the
  work surface
with newspapers.
Tie a temporary
string hanger onto
the ornament.

3 Place desired
  paint colors on
a plate. To make
large dots, dip the
eraser end of a
pencil into the
paint and dot onto
the ornament. If
desired, sprinkle
with glitter. To
make small dots,
use the end of a
toothpick or the
handle end of a
paintbrush. Let dry.

4 Glue sequin
  string around
the ornament top.
Let the glue dry.
Use a 10-inch
piece of ribbon
to make the
permanent hanger.
Tie into a bow or
knot as desired.

jack-o'- lantern ornament

supplies

Round white or
  orange glass
  ornament
Pencil; newspapers
Thick white crafts
  glue

Glitter in black
  or pink
1/8- to 1/4-inch-wide
  ribbon

what to do

1 Gently draw a
  pumpkin face
on the ornament
using pencil. Press
lightly so as not to
break the ornament.

2 Cover work
  surface with
newspapers. Draw
on facial features
using glue. While
wet, sprinkle on
glitter. Let dry.

3 Tie a ribbon
  bow at the top.

starry night ornament

supplies

Round orange
  glass ornament
Drinking glass
Gems in round and
  star shapes in
  clear and orange
Thick white
  crafts glue
Black and gold
  cording

what to do

1 Set the
  ornament in
the glass while
working on
one side.

2 Glue gems to
  the ornament
as desired. Let dry.
Turn the ornament
over. Glue gems to
the remaining side.
Let the glue dry.

3 Wrap and glue
  cord around the
top. Let dry. Add a
cord hanger.

spider-'n'- web ornament

supplies

1/4-inch-wide
  rubber bands
Round orange
  glass ornament
Newspapers
Black spray paint
5 inches of orange
  sequins on a string
Spider ring
1/8-inch-wide satin
  ribbon

what to do

1 Place a rubber band around the center of the ornament. Place a second band over the topper and around the bottom (the bands will cross in the center). Place two rubber bands between those already on the ornament, making sure all intersect in the same place.

2 In a well-ventilated area, cover work surface with newspapers. Spray-paint a light coat over the ornament. Let dry. Remove the bands.

3 Glue the sequin string around the top. Let dry. Add a spider ring and ribbon hanger.

halloween swirl ornament

supplies

Round clear glass ornament with removable topper
Newspapers
Acrylic paints in black, yellow, and orange
Thick white crafts glue
2-inch piece of rhinestone trim
1-inch-wide metallic ribbon

what to do

1 Remove the topper from the ornament. Set the topper aside.

2 Cover work surface with newspapers. Put small amounts of black, orange, and yellow paints into the ornament. Rotate the ornament so the paints swirl together and the entire inside is covered with paint. Leave the topper off and let dry.

3 Place the topper on the ornament. Glue the rhinestone trim around the ornament top, trimming to fit. Let the glue dry. Thread the ribbon through the ornament top for a hanger.

boo-to-you ornament

supplies

Round white glass ornament
Glass paints in black, purple, green, yellow, and orange
Paintbrush
Needle-nose pliers
12-inch-long piece of lead-free solder
Clear silicone glue
Ribbon (optional)

what to do

1 Gently wash and dry the glass ornament. Avoid touching the areas on the ornament that will be painted.

2 Looking at the pattern, *above,* as a guide, paint the word "BOO" and the exclamation point in black. Let the paint dry.

3 Add the colored accents as shown, leaving a black border. Let the paint dry.

4 Use a needle-nose pliers to curl the ends of the solder. Form one end over the B on the ornament and carefully wrap the ornament top with the solder. Glue the solder in place. Let the glue dry. To hang, use the top solder loop or add a ribbon.

bewitching trims

Just minutes before you open the door to Halloween guests, make these striking candles and ornaments using wax stickers. Just peel and press and you're ready to entertain with creepy, clever trims throughout your very own haunted house.

creepy candles

supplies
Candle wax stickers in Halloween designs
Candles in a variety of shapes, sizes, and colors
Raffia, if desired

what to do
1 Decide the desired placement of the wax stickers.

2 Carefully peel off the wax shapes from the paper. Position them gently on the candles, pressing in place until the shapes adhere to the candles.

3 Tie a raffia bow around the candle bottom if desired. Remove the raffia when burning the candle.

terrifying trim

supplies
Candle wax stickers in bat or other desired designs
Round white glass ornament
¼-inch-wide ribbon
Scissors

what to do
1 Carefully peel off the wax shapes from the paper. Position them gently on the ornament, pressing in place until the shapes adhere.

2 Add a ribbon hanger to the ornament top. Trim the ribbon ends.

holiday greetings wreath

Set a magical mood by making this quick and inexpensive wreath to welcome all the little folks on Beggars' Night. All it takes are white pony beads sprinkled between twists of colored chenille sticks to add Halloween sparkle to a grapevine wreath coated in glossy black paint.

supplies

Newspapers
24-inch grapevine wreath
Black, glossy spray paint
Chenille stems in orange, silver, and black
Round pencil
Scissors
White pony beads
1 yard of 2-inch-wide silver wired-edge ribbon

what to do

1 In a well-ventilated area, cover the work surface with newspapers. Lay the grapevine wreath on the newspapers and spray-paint one side of the wreath using black glossy paint. Let the paint dry. Turn the wreath over and spray-paint the back side. Let the paint dry.

2 Shape several orange and silver chenille stems into coils or S-shapes as shown in the photograph, *opposite*. Arrange the coils and S-shapes on the wreath and secure by wrapping one end of each chenille stem around a vine on the wreath.

3 To make each long spiral, wrap an orange chenille stem around a pencil. Remove the spiral from the pencil and tuck it into the wreath where desired, securing under the vines. Make six or seven spirals and attach them to the wreath.

4 Cut several 2-inch pieces from black chenille stems. Thread a white pony bead on each chenille stem piece. Twist each beaded chenille stem piece around the vine wreath. Continue adding beads between the chenille shapes until the desired look is achieved.

5 Decide where the bow will be placed on the wreath. Slip the piece of ribbon under some of the vines where the bow is desired. Tie the ribbon into a bow. Trim the ribbon ends as needed.

Light up the night with these glistening votive candleholders. Just about any small glass container will work—just add a touch of paint and a sprinkle of glitter.

very scary candleholders

supplies
Tracing paper
Pencil
Scissors
Votive
  candleholders or
  any small glass
  containers
Masking tape
Yellow glass paint
Paintbrush
Decoupage
  medium
Glitter in orange,
  green, and black

what to do

1 Trace the moon, star, and jack-o'-lantern patterns at *right* onto tracing paper. Cut out each pattern or grouping about ½ inch from the edge of the design.

2 Wash and dry the glass container. Avoid touching the areas to be painted. Tape the desired pattern inside the glass container. Using the pattern as a guide, paint inside the shapes using glass paint. Let the paint dry. Bake the glass item in the oven if directed by paint instructions.

3 Coat the outer surface of the glass container with decoupage medium, except the painted areas and the bottom of the container. Sprinkle glitter over the wet decoupage medium until well covered. Let it dry.

4 Brush off the excess glitter and put a light final coat of decoupage medium over the glittered areas only. Do not submerse the votive holder in water.

MOON PATTERN

STAR PATTERN

JACK-O'-LANTERN PATTERN

Cut from car window film, these shapes cling to glass to create a clever haunted house. Stored properly, they can be reused year after year.

spooky window scene

supplies
**Static cling black
  window film for
  car glass
Permanent black
  marking pen
Scissors
Cutting board
Crafts knife**

what to do

1 Using a marking
pen, trace the
patterns, *below*
and *pages 78–79,*
onto the film. Cut
out the shapes
with scissors.

2 On a cutting
board, use a
crafts knife to cut
out the inside
details. If it is
difficult to see the
drawn lines, slip a
piece of white paper
between the cutting
board and the film
before cutting.

3 Apply the film
pieces to a
window by gently
rubbing each film
piece to remove
the bubbles. If
necessary, wipe

the window with a
damp rag to help
the film stick.

4 To remove the
cutouts, gently
peel the film off the
window. To store

the pieces, keep
them separate with
sheets of paper
between them and
store flat.

GHOST
PATTERN

JACK-O'-
LANTERN
PATTERN

PUMPKIN
PATTERN

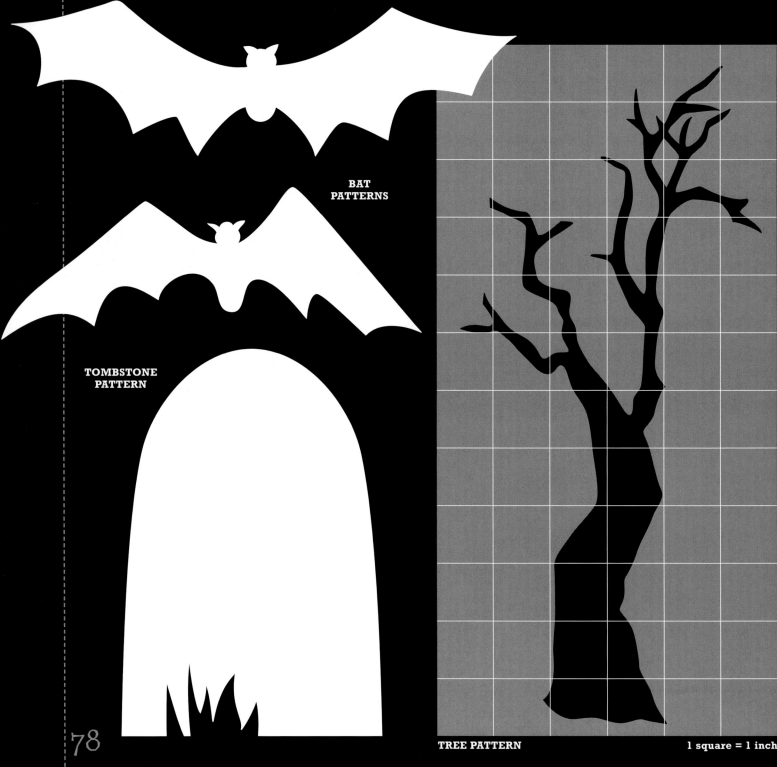

BAT
PATTERNS

TOMBSTONE
PATTERN

TREE PATTERN

1 square = 1 inch

1 square = 1 inch

roly-poly pumpkin trio

These jesterlike characters bring lots of giggles as they teeter with the slightest touch. Their chenille stem arms let you bend them into all sorts of funny poses.

supplies

Pencil
Tracing paper
Scissors; compass
Two 7-inch squares of green-and-black plaid fabric
7x7-inch piece of paper-backed fusible web
¼ yard of orange-and-black checked fabric
2-inch-diameter wood knob with flat side
Two 1½-inch-diameter wood knobs, each with one flat side
Acrylic paints in orange and black
Paintbrush
Heavy black thread
Sewing needle
Polyester fiberfill
Hot-glue gun and hot-glue sticks
3 chenille stems
Liquid seam sealant
3½-inch-long straw broom
5 yards of 30-gauge florist's wire
T-pin

what to do

1 Trace the leaf patterns, *right,* onto tracing paper. Cut out. For small body pattern, use a compass and draw a circle 6¾ inches across onto tracing paper and cut out. For the large body pattern, draw a circle 8¼ inches across onto tracing paper and cut out.

2 To make the leaves, fuse the green-and-black fabric squares together using fusible web.

3 From orange-and-black fabric, use patterns to cut one large body, two small bodies, and one 1⅛×12½-inch strip, and two 1⅛×10½-inch strips for arms. From double-sided fabric, cut 5 large and 10 small leaves.

4 Paint the knobs orange. Let dry.

With flat sides down, paint faces on the knobs, using the patterns, *right,* as a guide. Let dry.

5 For each body, use a double strand of heavy thread to sew a running stitch ¼ inch from edge of fabric. Stuff with fiberfill. Pull threads and knot.

6 For leaves, make a tuck in rounded end, glue to neck. Hot-glue heads to bodies.

7 For arms, cut chenille stems into one 10-inch-long and two 8-inch-long pieces. Apply liquid seam sealant to short ends of orange-and-black fabric strips. Let dry. Press under ¼ inch on one long side of each fabric strip. Tie a knot ½ inch from one end of each fabric strip. Push one end of

long chenille stem up against the knot of the long fabric strip. Wrap fabric around chenille stem with pressed edge covering raw edge. Slip-stitch closed. Tie a knot in the remaining end of the fabric strip ½ inch from the end, working the knot down against the end of the chenille stem. Repeat, using the shorter fabric strips and chenille stems.

8 To attach arms, center the longer arm behind the head and underneath the leaves of the larger body. Shape arms to fit curve of head. Glue in place. Attach the arms to the small figures in the same manner.

9 Glue the broom to a character as desired. Let dry.

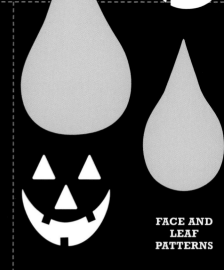

FACE AND LEAF PATTERNS

10 For tendrils, cut florist's wire into twelve 15-inch-long pieces. To curl the wire, wrap each piece around a pencil. Slip off pencil. Apply glue to one end of a tendril and slip it between the leaves, pressing the end into the body. Glue three tendrils around each head. Use a T-pin to make a small hole about ¼ inch deep in the top of each head. Glue one tendril to the top of each head.

81

wiggling witch

Crank up the "Monster Mash" and give this gal a tap! With a funnel used for a body, this happy-go-lucky witch will bob to the beat and have you smiling in no time.

supplies

Two 6x$\frac{1}{2}$-inch wood dowels
Acrylic paints in black, orange, and purple
Paintbrush
2 wood hearts approximately 2x1x$\frac{3}{16}$ inches
1x$\frac{1}{2}$-inch wood dowel
Hot-glue gun and hot-glue sticks
Small wood base
Paint pens in black, green, orange, and glitter gold
Scissors
4-inch plastic funnel
Black spray paint
Tracing paper
Pencil
Sheet of white card stock
Permanent marking pens in black, and green
Red colored pencil
Thick white crafts glue
Scrap of yellow paper

what to do

1 For legs, paint the 6-inch-long dowels with orange and purple stripes. Paint the hearts black for shoes. Let the paint dry.

2 Hot-glue the bottom of each dowel to the center back of one heart. The pointed portion of the heart becomes the toe of the shoe. Hot-glue the legs together by gluing the 1×½-inch wood dowel spacer between the top of each leg. Hot-glue the shoes to the wood base. Use glitter gold to squeeze three gold buttons down the center of each shoe.

3 With heavy-duty scissors, cut the handle from the funnel if necessary. Spray-paint the funnel black and set aside to dry.

4 Trace the patterns, *right,* onto tracing paper and cut out. Cut the front (with chin) and the back (without chin) head pieces from card stock. Color the hat black using marking pen. Use green to color the hair as shown, *right,* for front. For back, color entire head area with green. Draw in face details using black. Color the mouth and cheeks with red pencil. Outline the hat with black paint pen. Add a gold hat band. Add strokes of green and gold to hair.

5 Cut a length of card stock to go around the neck of the funnel. Color it with black. Glue strip around neck of funnel. Glue

head front to one side of tube and head back to the opposite side.

6 Cut arms from card stock. Color the sleeves black and add orange paint-pen stripes to each cuff area. Outline the stripes with black paint pen. Let the paint dry.

7 Use crafts glue to glue the arms to the sides of the body. Add buttons down the front of the body using glitter gold paint pen.

8 Cut stars from yellow paper and glue the large one to coat and the small one to the tip of each hat.

HAT STAR PATTERN

COAT STAR PATTERN

FRONT/BACK HEAD AND HAT PATTERN

ARM PATTERN

83

Serve up
delicious
concoctions on
a wood tray
touting an inlay
of small broken
tiles in the shape
of a pumpkin.

mosaic pumpkin tray

supplies

Tracing paper
Pencil
Scissors
15x11x3-inch
  wood serving
  tray
Safety glasses
Crafting mosaic
  tiles: 2 bags of
  orange, 2 bags of
  green, and 3
  bags of white
Tile-cutting
  nipper
Hammer
Towels
Crafts stick
Mosaics adhesive
Mosaics white
  sanded tile grout
Spatula
Rag or sponge
Green acrylic
  paint
Paintbrush
Satin varnish

what to do

1 Enlarge and trace the pumpkin pattern, *below,* onto tracing paper. Cut out the pattern.

2 Place the pattern in the center of the tray and trace around the shape.

3 Put on safety glasses before breaking tiles. Cut tiles into various shapes with a cutting nipper and hammer. To break tiles with a hammer, put them on a towel with the colored surface down. Cover with a towel and strike with a hammer.

4 Use a crafts stick to spread adhesive on small sections of the wood at a time. Glue orange tile chips inside the pumpkin outline. chips for the stem and to form a border around the edge of the tray bottom. Fill in the remaining spaces with white tile chips.

5 Mix the grout according to the manufacturer's instructions. Spread grout on the top of the tiles with a spatula and your fingers, pressing the grout in spaces between tiles. Wipe grout off the top of tiles with a damp sponge or rag. Let it set up.

6 Paint the tray green. Let it dry. Apply a coat of varnish over the paint. Let it dry.

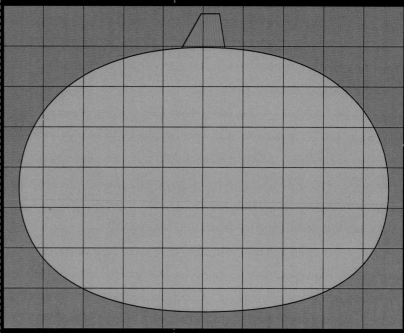

PUMPKIN PATTERN

1 square = 1 inch

jack-o'-lantern centerpiece

Any type of jack-o'-lantern, carved or made of foam, will take on a bewitching personality when topped with this star-struck hat. The purchased hat is embellished with purple and orange glitter. Placed on a handful of shredded mylar, this clever creation makes a stunning centerpiece. For extra shrieks, place a plastic lizard or frog on the brim.

supplies

Tracing paper
Pencil
Scissors
White pencil
Witch hat
Lime green paint pen
Thick white crafts glue
Paintbrush
Glitter in purple and orange
Foam or carved jack-o'-lantern
Shredded mylar
Plastic lizard or frog

what to do

1 Trace star patterns, *right,* and cut out. Use white pencil to trace around star shapes on witch hat.

2 Use a lime green paint pen to draw over star shapes. Let the paint pen dry.

3 Paint a thin coat of crafts glue inside each drawn star shape. While the glue is wet, sprinkle it with the desired color of glitter. Let it dry and shake off the excess glitter.

4 Place jack-o'-lantern on a handful of shredded mylar. Arrange the hat on top of the jack-o'-lantern, adding a plastic lizard or frog to the brim.

SMALL STAR PATTERN

LARGE STAR PATTERN

ghoulish garlands

Whatever the theme of your Halloween decorating, you'll find a garland that fits right into the plan. From funky witch hats to gem-embellished masks and dancing candy corn with pony bead spacers—these festive trims will add holiday pizzazz to doors, mantels, windows, banisters, and more!

supplies
Tracing paper
Pencil
Scissors
White pencil
Crafting foam in
  orange, yellow,
  white, purple,
  green, and black
Round and
  star-shape paper
  punches
Pinking shears
Thick white crafts
  glue
Gems
Permanent silver
  marking pen
Plastic-coated
  colored wires
Chenille stems
Curling ribbon
Pony beads
Ice pick

what to do

1. Trace the desired garland patterns from *pages 90–91* onto tracing paper. Cut out shapes.

2. Trace around patterns as many times as desired on crafting foam. If pencil lines do not show up, use a white pencil. Cut out shapes.

3. To make tiny circle or star shapes, punch out with a paper punch. To make zigzag stripes, cut with a pinking shears.

4. Layer and glue pieces together, using the patterns as a guide. Let the glue dry.

5. Embellish the foam pieces by adding gems, small snippets of foam, or by drawing in details with silver marking pen.

6. To connect the garland pieces, use the photographs, *opposite* and *above,* for ideas. Use a paper punch to add holes if needed. Thread wire, chenille stems, or curling ribbon through the holes, adding beads if desired. To form wire into a spiral shape, wrap it around an ice pick before connecting it to foam shapes.

continued on page 90

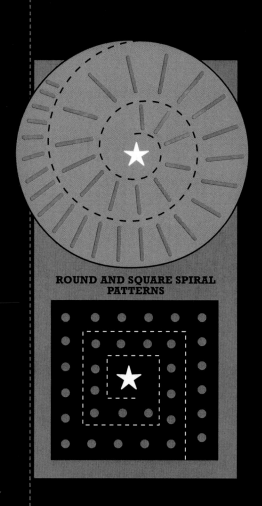

ROUND AND SQUARE SPIRAL PATTERNS

CANDY CORN PATTERN

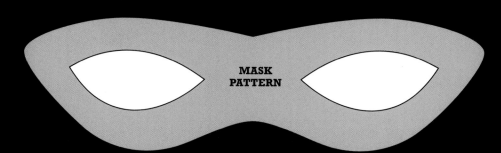

MASK PATTERN

BOO!

BOO LETTERING PATTERN

BOO LETTERING PATTERN

SQUATTY WITCH HAT
PATTERN

TALL WITCH HAT
PATTERN

91

When the chilly October winds blow, let this colorful trim catch each gust. The Halloween wind sock is stitched using several colors of yarn and simple stitches that work quickly over 7-count plastic canvas. The nylon streamers are edged with sequins on a string that sparkles even when the moon is shining.

supplies

Red Heart Super Saver worsted weight yarn in kiwi (651), bright yellow (324), black (312), lavender (358), white (311), and vibrant orange (354)
No. 13 tapestry needle
7-count plastic canvas, cut 85 holes × 35 holes
Cotton embroidery floss in black and white
Scissors
Hot-glue gun and hot-glue sticks
1 yard of black nylon fabric
Cutting mat
Rotary cutter
Ruler
Approximately 20 yards of orange and black sequins on a string

what to do

1 Following the chart on *page 95,* stitch the design on plastic canvas using the continental stitch. Do not stitch the first four columns of the left edge of the design. Start in the fifth hole at the top left, beginning with the fifth stitch. Stitch all French knots using four strands of floss.

2 After stitching is completed, except for the four left columns, fold the plastic canvas to form a tube. Overlap the four columns of holes on each end and finish stitching the design, going through both layers of canvas to join the ends.

continued on page 94

93

3 Overcast the top and the bottom edges using black yarn.

4 Cut two 30-inch lengths from orange, kiwi, and black yarns. Tie the yarns together on one end and divide the yarns into the two yarns of each color. Braid together for 17 inches. Tie the yarns together at the end of the braid and trim any excess yarn. Glue one end inside the top of the plastic canvas tube and glue the other end on the opposite side to form a hanger.

5 Spread nylon fabric on the cutting mat. Use a rotary cutter to cut the fabric into 10 lengthwise strips that are 2 inches wide. Stop cutting 1 inch from the top edge. Apply glue along the long sides and press sequins along edge. Let the glue dry. Apply glue along the bottom inside edge of the plastic canvas tube $\frac{1}{2}$ inch from the bottom. Glue the top edge of the nylon streamers to the tube.

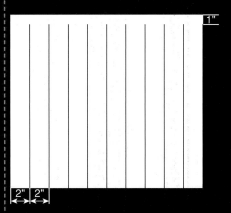

NYLON FABRIC CUTTING DIAGRAM

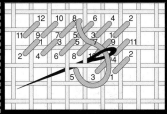

CONTINENTAL STITCH

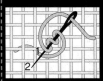

FRENCH KNOT

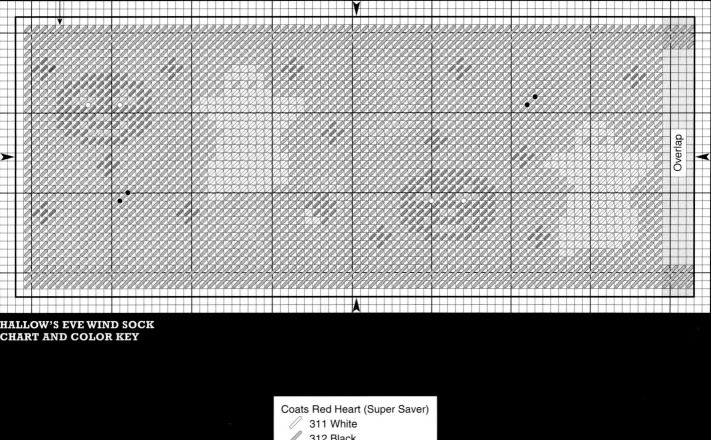

HALLOW'S EVE WIND SOCK
CHART AND COLOR KEY

Coats Red Heart (Super Saver)
- 311 White
- 312 Black
- 324 Bright yellow
- 354 Vibrant orange
- 358 Lavender
- 651 Kiwi

FRENCH KNOT
- ○ 000 DMC White
- ● 310 DMC Black

clever

Get in the spirit

costumes

crazy caterpillar

For a group of young friends, this prizewinning costume gives getting together a whole new meaning. Created from a length of lime green felt, the caterpillar's coat is decorated with bright, irregular spots.

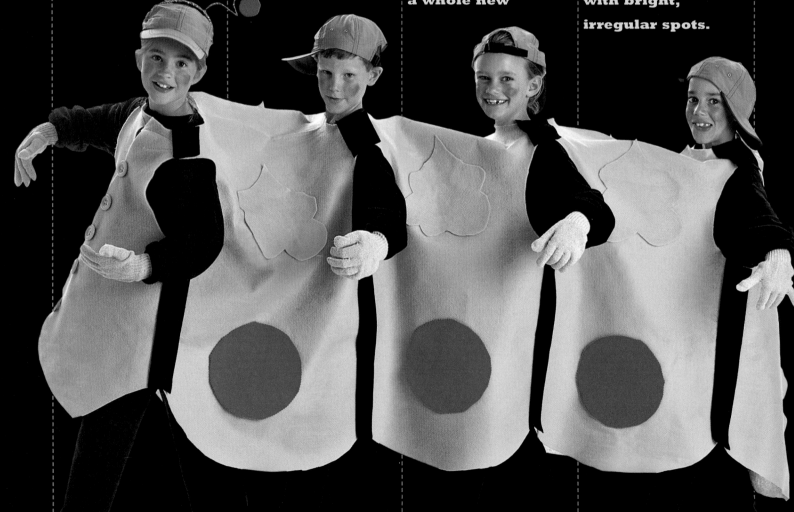

supplies

Paper; pencil
Tape measure
2½ yards of
72-inch-wide
lime green felt
Scissors
Large yellow
buttons
Sewing needle
Thread
½ yard of
72-inch-wide
black felt
Thick white crafts
glue
½ yard of
72-inch-wide
each of pink and
yellow felt
Pinking shears
Tracing paper
Headband
Metallic chenille
stems
Two large pink
pom-poms
Purchased black
pants and
sweatshirts, white
tennis shoes, and
green baseball
hats and gloves

what to do

1 Use paper to make an oval arm opening pattern, 12 inches high and 6 inches wide. Make a circular 6-inch-diameter neck opening pattern.

2 Fold green felt in half lengthwise as shown on the diagram, *page 100.* Use the patterns to start marking the neck holes 4 inches from the front end at the fold. Leaving 18 inches between neck holes, mark the remaining three neck holes. Cut out the four neck holes.

3 For each arm opening, trace around the pattern 4 inches from the neck opening. Cut out the eight arm holes.

4 Cut scallops across bottom, from centers of armholes as shown in the diagram on *page 100*. Cut front into a vest shape and angle the back to create the look of a tail.

5 Overlap front vest pieces and secure by sewing on large buttons. Stitch back seam.

6 Cut eight 4x24-inch strips from black felt. Glue strips below armholes, trimming to match the bottom scallop.

7 Cut six 8½-inch circles from pink felt using pinking shears. Enlarge and trace the pattern, *page 101.* Use the pattern to cut six shapes from yellow felt using scissors. Glue the cutouts as shown, *left.*

8 For antennae, wrap chenille stems around a headband. Glue pom-poms to ends of two stems and wrap around sides of headband. Place over the hat of the leader.

continued on page 100

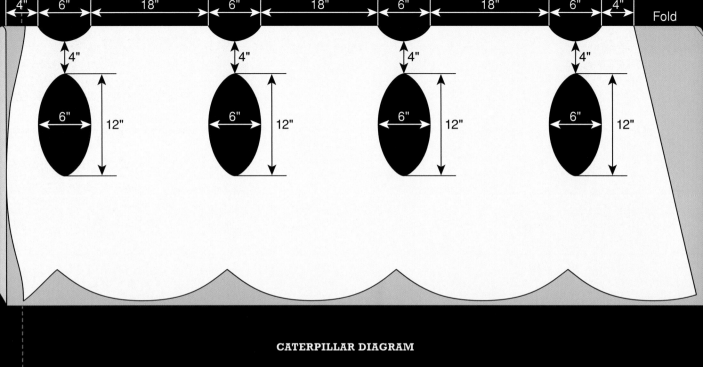

CATERPILLAR DIAGRAM

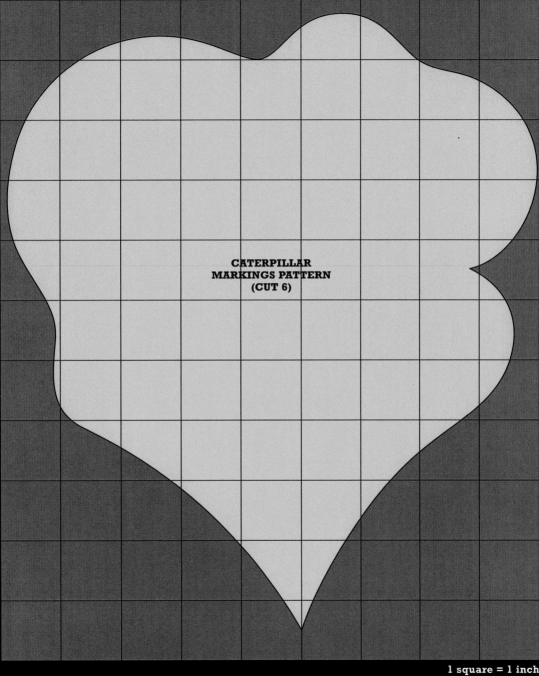

CATERPILLAR
MARKINGS PATTERN
(CUT 6)

1 square = 1 inch

cleopatra

Look like the queen of Egypt herself with this golden costume embellished with gems of all colors. An elegant gold doily, dripping with beads, adds the crowning touch.

supplies

Scissors
3 yards of 45-inch-wide metallic knit fabric with sequins
Thread
Sewing needle
Two 9-inch pieces of $\frac{1}{2}$-inch-wide elastic
1 yard of 45-inch-wide quilted lamé
4 yards of $\frac{1}{2}$-inch-wide sequin trim
Fabric glue
Assorted acrylic gems; gem glue
1 yard of $\frac{1}{4}$-inch-wide grosgrain ribbon
$1\frac{1}{4}$ yards of 4-inch-wide sequined elastic
4 yards of gold beads on a string
8-inch-diameter gold crocheted doily
1 yard of 2-inch-wide sequined elastic
Sandals
Glitter
face paint

1 Cut an 8-inch neck opening in the center of the metallic knit fabric. Fold the fabric piece in half, right sides together, with the short ends meeting. Sew the side seams, allowing 10-inch arm openings and 10-inch bottom slits on both sides. Turn.

2 Along each shoulder, stretch and stitch a 9-inch piece of elastic to the inside of the garment.

3 For collar, use the diagram on *page 104* as a guide to cut a 17-inch-diameter circle from lamé. Cut a 5-inch-diameter circle in the center for neck opening. Cut center back open. Topstitch a tiny hem around all edges. Glue the sequin trim to collar edge. Add gems to the collar where desired. Stitch ribbons to each corner of the center back opening for ties.

4 For belt apron, enlarge and trace pattern from *page 105*. Cut the shape from gold lamé. Glue the trim and gems to the belt apron as shown in the photographs, *above*. Cut the 4-inch-wide sequined elastic to a comfortable waist measurement plus seams. Stitch the apron to the center front of 4-inch-wide sequined elastic belt. Stitch center back seam of belt.

5 For headpiece, cut the beaded string into ten equal pieces. Sew five to each side of doily as shown, *opposite*. Glue on gems as desired. Let the glue dry.

6 To make upper arm bands, cut 2-inch-wide sequined elastic two inches larger than upper arm measurement. Sew a 1-inch seam, tacking ends to back of elastic.

continued on page 104

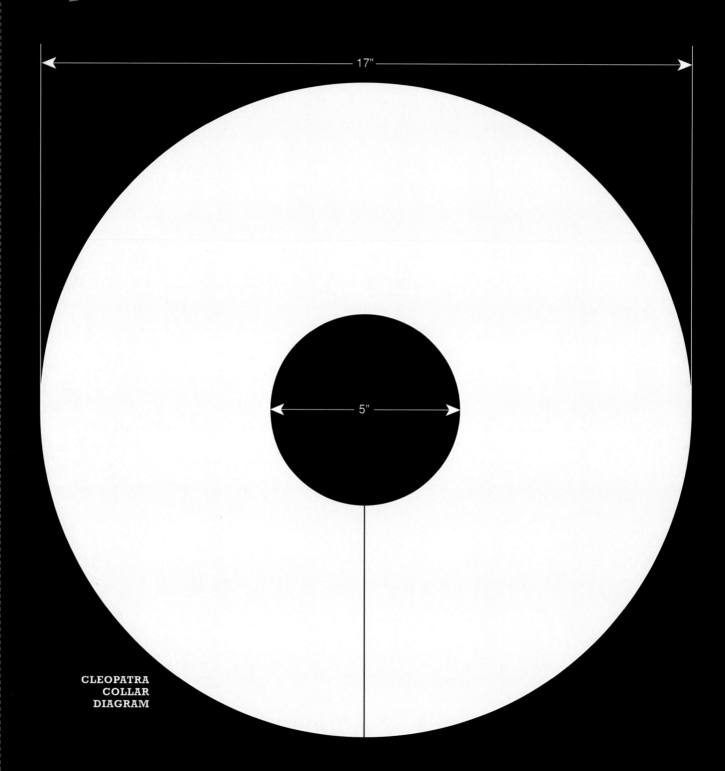

17"

5"

CLEOPATRA
COLLAR
DIAGRAM

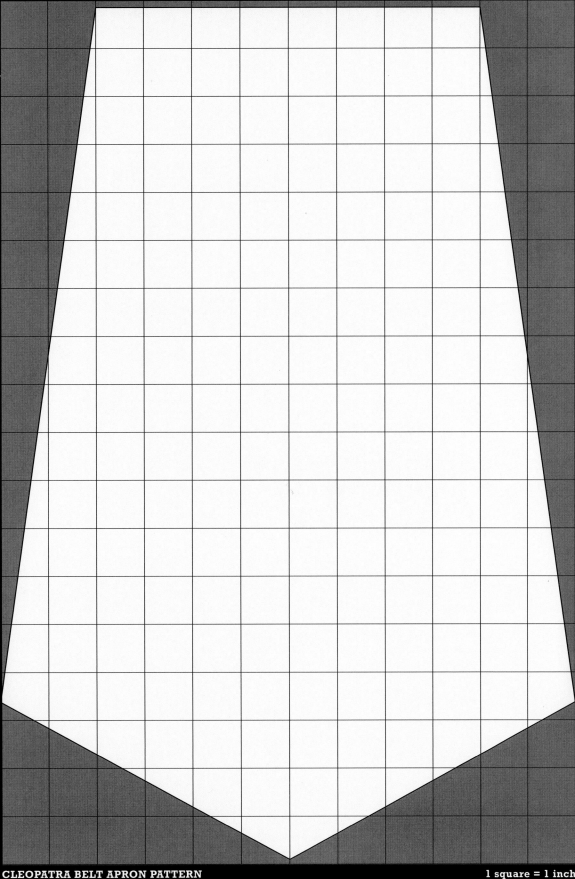

CLEOPATRA BELT APRON PATTERN

1 square = 1 inch

look-at-me costumes

A smart alternative to a mask, this little mouse has a painted face made from supplies around the house. Add easy-sew ears to a headband to complete the look.

Let a child's imagination soar with a lofty costume created from a recycled box.

Or, create a caveman with fake fur and spray paint.

squeaky the mouse

supplies

For costume:
Tracing paper
  Pencil
    Scissors
      ⅓ yard gray felt
      9x12-inch piece of pink felt
      Thick white crafts glue
      Chenille stem
Stapler
1 yard pink baby rickrack
White plastic headband
Hot-glue gun and hot-glue sticks
Small, natural sponge

White acrylic paint
Gray hooded sweat suit

For face paints:
1 teaspoon cornstarch
½ teaspoon cold cream
Mixing bowl
½ teaspoon water
Muffin tin
Food coloring
Small paintbrush or cotton swab

what to do

1 Enlarge and trace the mouse ear patterns, *right,* and cut out. Cut two outer ears from gray felt. Cut two inner ears from pink felt.

2 Glue an inner ear atop each outer ear, sandwiching half of a chenille stem between. Tuck each ear, securing with a staple along the bottom edge. Glue rickrack around the outer edge of each inner ear.

3 Cut a strip of gray felt the length and width of the headband. Glue the strip around the top of the headband, trimming as necessary to match the edges. Bend the bottom 1 inch of each ear forward at a 90-degree angle. Hot-glue the bent portion of each ear to the underside of the headband.

4 Dip a moist sponge into a puddle of white paint; sponge-paint the gray on the ears and headband. Let the paint dry.

5 For face paint, stir together the cornstarch and cold cream in a mixing bowl until it is well blended. Add water and stir.

6 Decide how many colors of paint you want. Put a dab of the cold cream mixture into a muffin tin for each color. Add food coloring, one drop at a time, until the desired colors are achieved. Mix well.

7 Using the photograph, *opposite,* for inspiration, paint the cheeks and nose using a paintbrush or cotton swab. Add whiskers and other details as desired.

flying high airplane

supplies

Cardboard box appropriate for the size of the child
Duct tape
Utility knife
Tracing paper
Pencil
Extra flat pieces of cardboard
Hot-glue gun and hot-glue sticks
Plastic margarine tub
Newspapers
Spray paint in desired color
4x4x1-inch piece of wood
Drill and drill bit
Bolt slightly longer than margarine tub depth and a nut
Colored electrical tape
Two 30-inch-long pieces of 1½-inch fabric strapping

continued on page 108

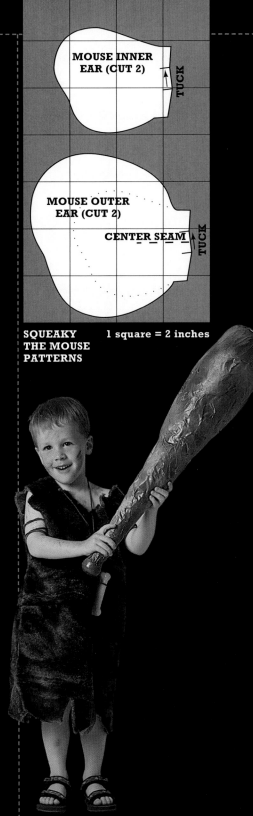

MOUSE INNER EAR (CUT 2)

TUCK

MOUSE OUTER EAR (CUT 2)

CENTER SEAM

TUCK

SQUEAKY THE MOUSE PATTERNS

1 square = 2 inches

what to do

1 Fold flaps from the box bottom to the inside and tape in place. Fold the two side flaps from the top to the inside and tape in place. Using a utility knife, trim semicircles from the two remaining flaps to allow a child to stand in the box.

2 Enlarge and trace the plane patterns, *opposite*. Cut the shapes from cardboard.

3 Use hot-glue to attach the tail top to the center of the tail. Glue the two tail supports perpendicular to the underneath side of the tail, each about 2 inches from the center. Glue two supports to the underside of each wing, aligning with the outside edge as shown in the photo on *page 106*. With

straight sides aligned, glue the propellers to the propeller center. Glue the propeller unit to the bottom of the margarine tub. Let all glue set.

4 In a well-ventilated area, cover your work surface with newspapers. Spray-paint all sides of the box and cardboard pieces. Let the paint dry.

5 Assemble the airplane using hot-glue and according to the photograph. To add the propeller, back it with the wood square inside the box. Drill a hole through the box and wood piece. Drill a hole in the center of the propeller. Secure in place with a nut and bolt.

6 Add stripes to the airplane as desired using electrical tape.

7 Cut two 1½-inch-long slits in each untaped box flap for shoulder straps. Insert the ends of the strapping through the slits. Adjust to fit child and knot the ends of the strapping.

tough-guy caveman

supplies

Spray paint in black, gray, and brown
⅞ yard of 60-inch-wide gray fake fur
Scissors; gray sewing thread
Sewing needle
Three 1-yard-long strips of brown leather
Vinyl dog bone
Fat baseball bat
Newspaper
Masking tape
Sandals

what to do

1 Spray-paint fake fur with

stripes of gray and black as desired. Let the paint dry.

2 Cut a straight tunic front/back from painted fur. Cut a diamond shape in the center for the neck. Stitch side seams from bottom edge, leaving 10 inches open for each arm. Cut jagged points into the bottom.

3 For necklace, tie the center of one leather strip around one end of the bone. Knot ends.

4 For arm bands, tie leather strips in crisscross fashion around the upper arms. Tie the ends.

5 For club, pad bat with crumpled newspapers. Secure in place with masking tape. Wrap the entire bat with tape, covering the papers. Spray the club with gray and brown paint.

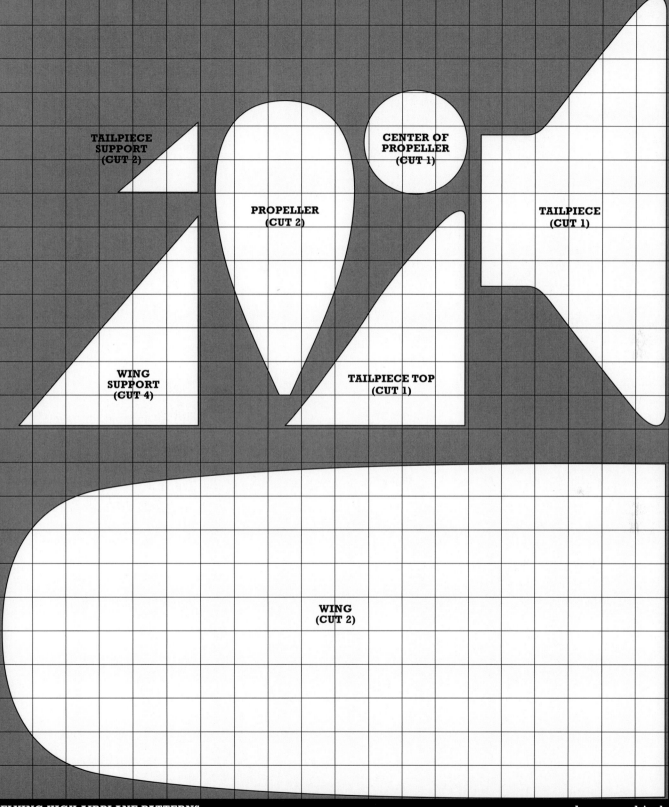

TAILPIECE
SUPPORT
(CUT 2)

PROPELLER
(CUT 2)

CENTER OF
PROPELLER
(CUT 1)

TAILPIECE
(CUT 1)

WING
SUPPORT
(CUT 4)

TAILPIECE TOP
(CUT 1)

WING
(CUT 2)

FLYING HIGH AIRPLANE PATTERNS

1 square = 1 inch

lu-lu the ladybug

Here's a last-minute costume idea that's cute as a bug! Wings made of crafting foam, and a purchased hat embellished with chenille stems and pom-pom antennae transform any little munchkin into a fun-loving, lu-lu of a ladybug.

supplies

Pencil
Tracing paper
Scissors
1/4-inch-thick red
  crafting foam
Thin black
  crafting foam
Hot-glue gun and
  hot-glue sticks
Paper punch
4 eyelets and
  eyelet punch
Pair of black
  42-inch-long
  shoelaces
Purchased red
  hat and black
  gloves
Black chenille
  stem
Two large, black
  pom-poms

what to do

1 Enlarge and trace the wing pattern, *page 113,* onto tracing paper. Cut out. Trace the dot pattern and cut out. Cut two wings from red foam and six dots from the black foam.

2 Using the diagram, *page 112,* glue the short flat edges of the wings together. Glue three dots on each wing. Let the glue dry.

3 Use a paper punch to make two holes at the top of each wing. For reinforcement, add an eyelet to each.

4 Tie the shoelaces together at one end. Place the knot by the seam on the wrong side of the wings. Thread the laces through the holes in each wing.

5 For hat, poke a chenille stem through the top of the hat. Glue a pom-pom on each end. Let dry.

continued on page 112

LADYBUG
PLACEMENT
DIAGRAM

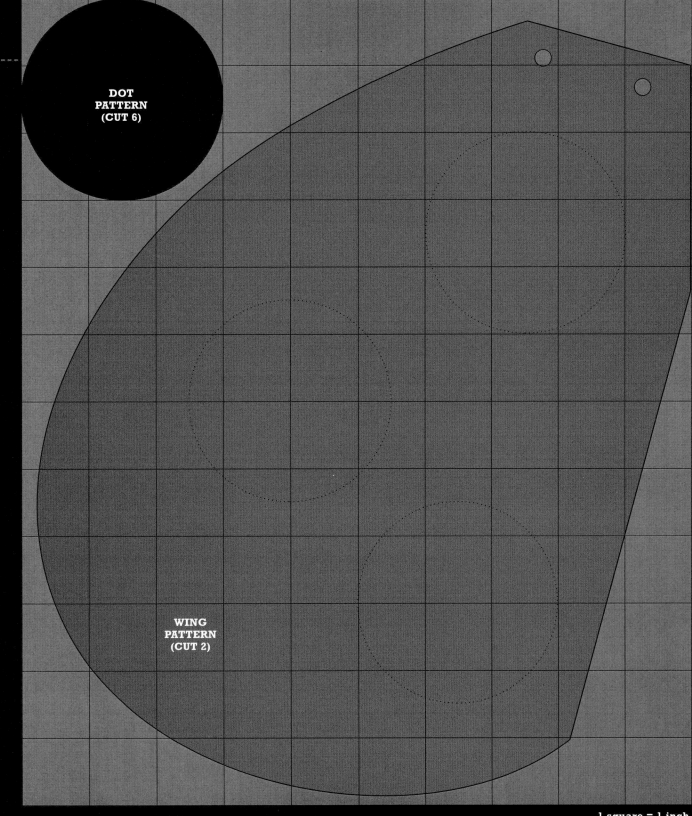

DOT PATTERN (CUT 6)

WING PATTERN (CUT 2)

1 square = 1 inch

115

A great Halloween costume no matter your age, this scarecrow seems to attract the birds rather than scare them away. Burlap patches and bits of raffia make this guy look like the real thing.

stanley scarecrow

supplies

Ruler; pencil
Fusible web paper
Scissors
**Burlap in red,
 yellow, and blue**
Bib overalls
Needle and thread
Straw hat

Raffia
Fine wire
**Small and large
 artificial crows**
Plaid shirt
**3 bandanna
 handkerchiefs**
**Face paints in
 black and red**
Eyeliner
Corncob pipe

what to do

1 To make patches, trace a 4-inch square onto web paper. Cut out and fuse to burlap. Cut burlap shapes 1 inch bigger on all sides. Fringe the outer edges. Arrange the patches on the overalls and fuse in place. Accent with running stitches if desired.

2 Trim hat with jagged cuts at the outer edge. Wire a band of raffia around the brim. Wire a small crow to the brim of the hat.

3 Hand-stitch raffia to the inside of the shirt cuffs and pant leg openings. Tuck bandannas into the bib pocket, shoulder strap, and back pocket. Wire the large crow to the top of an overall strap or around an arm.

4 Add face details such as red cheeks, eyebrows, and stitch marks using eyeliner and face paints. Tuck a corncob pipe in the bib pocket.

Step 1

Step 2

**RUNNING
STITCH**

115

frankie the monster

You'll be doing the monster mash in style with this silly mask made from shiny vinyl place mats. Throw on a flea market jacket and you're ready for loads of Halloween fun.

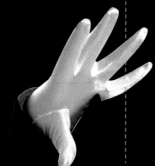

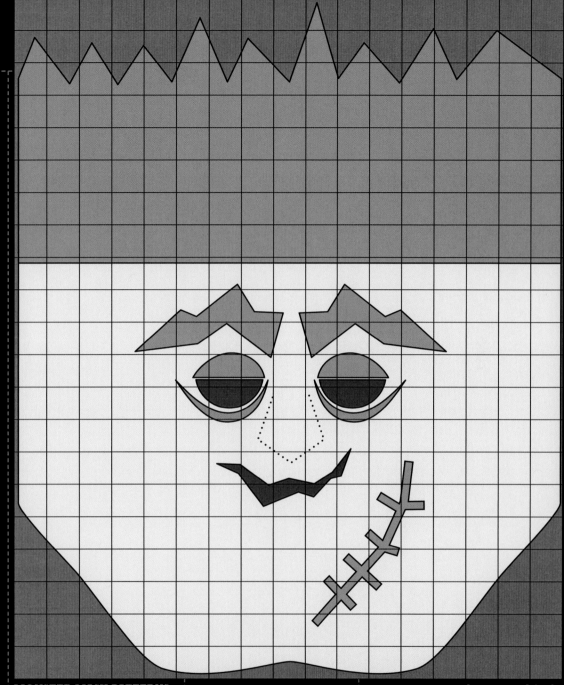

supplies
Pencil
Tracing paper
Scissors
Vinyl place mats
  or crafting foam
  in lavender and
  lime green
Crafts knife
Thick white
  crafts glue
Paper punch
Pair of shoelaces

what to do

1 Enlarge the face and hair patterns, *right.* Trace all patterns onto tracing paper and cut out. Cut the face from green vinyl material and the rest of the pattern pieces from lavender. Use a crafts knife to cut out the eyeholes, mouth, and nose. Use scissors to cut a 1-inch-high T for neck bolt. Cut a ½-inch-long slit to hold the neck bolt.

MONSTER MASK PATTERNS

1 square = 1 inch

2 Overlap and glue the hair to the top of the head. Glue all of the face pieces in place, using the pattern as a guide. Let dry.

3 In line with eyeholes, use a paper punch to make a hole 1 inch from each mask edge. Tie a shoelace through each hole. Tie the shoelaces behind head to secure in place.

117

clarise the clown

Get ready to put
on a happy face
with this cheerful
clown costume.
Bright fabrics
and rickrack
turn an ordinary
sweat suit into
circuslike attire.

supplies

Pencil
Fusible web paper
Assorted bright
  solids and
  polka-dot fabric
Scissors
Blue sweat suit
Thread
Needle
4x72-inch piece
  of bright fabric
5x72-inch piece
  of coordinating
  bright fabric
2 yards each of
  jumbo rickrack
  in two colors

1 yard of ⅜-inch-
  wide grosgrain
  ribbon
Purchased wig
Hairbands for cuffs
Face paints

what to do

1 Draw 4- and 5-inch-diameter circles onto web paper. Fuse to bright fabrics.

Cut out the fabric pieces and fuse to the sweatshirt and the sweatpants.

2 To make the collar, stitch a narrow hem on two short ends and one long side of each bright fabric rectangle. Topstitch rickrack to each of the long hemmed

edges. Layer the narrow strip on top of the wide strip with the right sides facing up. Stitch the raw edges together using a ¼-inch seam allowance. Press the seam open.

3 Gather along the seam to about 18 inches. Stitch the gathered edge onto the ribbon. Tie the collar around the neck.

119

all abuzz suits

Your little one will create quite a stir wearing these bold stripes. The tabard pattern could be easily enlarged for a matching adult version.

If you have only minutes to spare, make the cute frog getup, opposite. Just add the eyes and neck detail to a sweat suit and you're ready to go!

beatrice bee

supplies

Tracing paper
Pencil; scissors
24x48-inch piece
  of heavy sew-in
  interfacing
3 yards of 72-inch-
  wide black felt
¼ yard of 72-inch-
  wide yellow felt
Spray adhesive
Thick white crafts
  glue
6 yards of yellow
  medium rickrack
3 black loopy
  chenille stems
Black headband
Two 2-inch yellow
  pom-poms
Yellow gloves

what to do

1 Enlarge and trace patterns, *right*. Cut two tabards from interfacing and four from black felt. Cut two stingers from yellow felt.

2 Layer the interfacing tabards between felt tabards, using spray adhesive to temporarily secure layers. Machine-zigzag around neck and outer edges.

3 Cut six 3×22-inch yellow felt strips. Glue strips to tabard as indicated on pattern. Trim ends to match tabard. Glue yellow rickrack around neck and outer edges. Stitch an 18-inch-long piece of yellow rickrack to each side at the Xs to make ties.

4 Glue stinger points together, sandwiching one end of a chenille stem between. Stitch remaining end of chenille stem to dot on tabard back.

5 For antennae, twist one end of each remaining chenille stem around tip of headband. Glue a pom-pom to each tip. Let dry.

ready-to-leap frog

supplies

Scissors; ruler
¼ yard green felt
Fabric glue
Green hooded
  sweat suit, gloves,
  and swim fins
2 Ping-Pong
  balls
Permanent black
  marking pen

what to do

1 Cut nine 6-inch-long triangles from green felt. With narrow points down, glue around sweatshirt below hood. Let dry.

2 Cut two 4×7-inch pieces from felt. Align the center of one long edge with the center of a Ping-Pong ball. Shape and glue felt to ball at top and sides. Let dry.

3 Draw a dime-size dot in the middle of each Ping-Pong ball. Draw a slanted

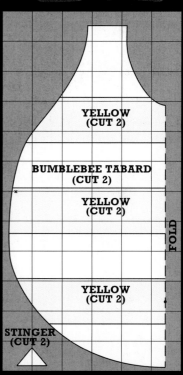

YELLOW
(CUT 2)

BUMBLEBEE TABARD
(CUT 2)

YELLOW
(CUT 2)

FOLD

YELLOW
(CUT 2)

STINGER
(CUT 2)

BEATRICE BEE PATTERNS   1 square = 2 inches

1-inch-long line through each dot.

4 Glue the eyes to top of the hood. Let dry.

121

chilling
Rattle those bones

parties

scare-me-silly party

From the moment they receive their imaginative invitations, party guests will know they're in for an unforgettable night of chills and little unexpected surprises. You can make the invites, right, using only a few supplies from around the house. And when it's time to quench the thirst of party-goers, be sure to fill the punch bowl with floating hands made by freezing fruit drink in a plastic glove.

cool ghoul treats

supplies
Clear plastic or latex gloves
Sugar-free flavored fruit drink mix
Gummy worms, optional
Twist ties
Paper towels
Cookie sheet
Scissors

what to do
1 If the gloves have a powdery residue inside, turn them inside out and soak in warm water or wipe with soapy water and rinse. Allow gloves to dry. Or, turn gloves inside out, leaving the powdery side to the outside.

2 Mix up fruit drink (sugar-free liquid freezes better than liquids with sugar) and pour into the gloves. If desired, add gummy worms to the juice before freezing. Add enough drink to fill gloves loosely but not so full that the fingers will not move. Fasten the gloves tightly with a twist tie. Place paper towels on a cookie sheet and lay the hands on the towels. Freeze.

3 When hands are frozen solid, cut off gloves with scissors. Float hands in a bowl of punch.

fun 'n' freaky invites

supplies for the cat invite
Tracing paper
Pencil
Scissors
Marking pens in silver and black
Craft paper in black, yellow, and white
Glue stick
4x5$\frac{1}{4}$-inch brown craft postcard
$\frac{3}{4}$-inch round red sticker

continued on page 126

what to do for the cat invite

1 Trace head and face patterns, *opposite,* onto tracing paper and cut out. The silver and black lines will be drawn with marking pens. Trace around head and center eye patterns on black paper, eyes on yellow, and teeth on white. Cut out.

2 Glue black head shape to center of postcard. Add yellow eyes, black pupils, and white teeth. Apply a red sticker to make the nose.

3 Use a black marking pen to draw in teeth lines, stars, dots, and swirls as shown on pattern. Use a silver pen to draw in whiskers and lines in eyes. Color in stars and one tooth. Add silver dots on top of

black dots and in the center of swirls.

4 Write party information on back side of card.

supplies for the skeleton invite

Tracing paper
Pencil
Scissors
Craft paper in black, white, orange, and yellow
Marking pens in silver and black
Glue stick
Round reinforcement stickers in yellow, purple, and green
Small round green stickers

what to do for the skeleton invite

1 Trace the patterns, *opposite,* onto tracing paper and cut out. The silver

and black lines will be drawn with marking pens. Fold a piece of black paper in half, bringing the short ends together. Trace around the card shape on the folded piece of black paper. Trace around the bow-tie shape on orange and the skeleton head on white. Cut out shapes. Cut a $3\frac{3}{4}\times\frac{5}{8}$-inch strip from yellow paper.

2 Glue the head shape approximately $\frac{1}{4}$ inch from the top of the card. Use the silver pen to draw in the arms and ribs.

3 Add small round and reinforcement stickers to the bow tie as desired. Trim or fold under stickers that hang over the edge of the bow tie. Glue the bow tie to the bottom of the head.

Glue the yellow paper strip to the bottom of the card.

4 Use a black pen to draw in face details and lettering. On the inside, write "And somewhere to go!" with a silver pen. Add the details to the eyes using the silver pen.

5 Write the invitation information on the inside of the card.

supplies for the "come if you dare" invite

$5\frac{1}{2}\times8\frac{1}{2}$-inch piece of purple paper
Glue stick
$3\frac{3}{4}\times5$-inch piece of black paper
Computer or magazines to make lettering
Computer paper
Scissors
Black marking pen

what to do for the "come if you dare" invite

1 Fold the purple paper in half, bringing the short ends together. Using the photo on *page 125* as a guide, glue the black piece of paper onto one side of the purple paper at an angle.

2 To make the words, use a computer to print each word in a different font. Make the word "please" approximately ¼ inch high. Make the remaining words and exclamation point between ½ and 1⅛ inches high. If a computer is not available, clip the letters or entire words from magazines. Glue the words in place.

3 Write the party information on the inside of card.

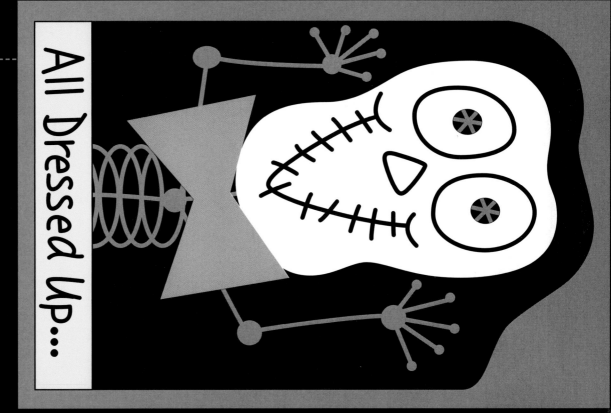

All Dressed Up...

SKELETON INVITE PATTERN

CAT INVITE PATTERN

a friendly fiends' feast

Gather around this enticing table filled with fanciful pumpkins and irresistible fare that will satisfy any goblin's appetite. The menu offers sausage links in cranberry sauce, sticks-and-stones snack mix, cookie wreaths crawling with edible spiders, delicious sandwiches, and a spritzed fruit drink that keeps cold with wiggle worm ice. For dessert try a shrunken head— a caramel apple trimmed with nuts and candies.

bubbling cranberry-sauced links

supplies
1 8-ounce can jellied cranberry sauce
$\frac{1}{3}$ cup catsup
1 tablespoon lemon juice
$\frac{1}{2}$ teaspoon dry mustard
$\frac{1}{8}$ teaspoon allspice
1 5.3-ounce package small fully cooked smoked sausage links

what to do
1 In a medium saucepan, stir together the cranberry sauce, catsup, lemon juice, dry mustard, and allspice. Cook and stir over medium heat until bubbly. Add the sausage links. Cover and cook over medium-low heat about 10 minutes or until heated through, stirring occasionally. Makes 8 servings.

Crockery cooker directions: Combine cranberry sauce, catsup, lemon juice, dry mustard, and allspice in a 1-quart crockery cooker. Stir in the smoked sausage links. Cover and cook for about 2 hours or until heated through.

continued on page 131

SHRUNKEN HEADS

shrunken heads

supplies

8 medium apples
8 wood sticks
Butter
1 cup coarsely chopped nuts, such as pecans, walnuts, or peanuts
21 ounces (about 75) vanilla caramels or chocolate caramels, unwrapped
3 tablespoons water
6 ounces vanilla-flavor candy coating
2 teaspoons shortening
Desired candies for decoration, such as licorice, candy corn, gumdrops, candy-coated chocolate pieces, optional
Tubes of writing gel decorating icing
Canned frosting

what to do

1 Wash and dry apples. Remove stems. Insert one wood stick into the stem end of each apple. Place apples on a buttered baking sheet. Place chopped nuts in a shallow dish; set aside.

2 In a heavy medium saucepan, heat and stir the caramels and water over medium-low heat just until caramels are melted.

3 Dip each apple into hot caramel mixture, spooning caramel evenly over apple. Allow excess caramel to drip off. Briefly set bottoms of apples in chopped nuts. Set apples on prepared baking sheet and let stand about 30 minutes or until firm.

4 In a heavy, small saucepan, heat and stir the vanilla-flavor candy coating and shortening over low heat just until mixture is melted. Holding apples over the saucepan, spoon the melted candy coating evenly over the tops of the caramel-coated apples. Return to baking sheet and let stand about 30 minutes or until firm.

5 Decorate the apples to resemble faces or monsters using desired candies and writing gel. Use writing gel or canned frosting to attach candies to dipped apples. Makes 8 medium apples.

To make ahead: Prepare apples as directed. Cover and chill for up to two days.

DRESSED-UP PUMPKINS

dressed-up pumpkins

supplies

Buttons
Acrylic gems in a variety of colors and shapes
Pumpkin
Towel
Thick white crafts glue
Ribbon
Purchased hat to fit pumpkin
Belt buckle

continued on page 133

SPRITZED FRUIT DRINK
WITH WIGGLE WORM ICE

SPIDERY COOKIE WREATHS

what to do

1 Using the photograph on *page 131* for ideas, decide arrangement of buttons and gems to make a face on pumpkin. Rest pumpkin on a towel so the side you wish to decorate is facing up. Glue the trims in place. Let the glue dry.

2 Measure a length of ribbon to fit around hat and add 2 inches. Cut ribbon. Weave one end through a belt buckle. Glue above brim. Let dry. Place hat on pumpkin. Glue in place if desired.

spritzed fruit drink with wiggle worm ice

supplies for fruit drink

1 12-ounce can frozen pineapple-orange juice concentrate

1 12-ounce can apricot nectar, chilled

2 12-ounce cans lemon-lime carbonated beverage, chilled

supplies for wiggle worm ice

1 6-ounce can frozen pineapple-orange juice concentrate

Snack-size, self-sealing plastic bags

Chewy, fruit-flavored candy worms

what to do for fruit drink

1 In a small punch bowl, prepare pineapple-orange juice concentrate according to package directions, using cold water. Stir in the apricot nectar. Add the carbonated beverage, stirring gently to mix.

Carefully add the wiggle worm ice.

what to do for wiggle worm ice

1 Prepare one 6-ounce can frozen pineapple-orange juice concentrate. Divide juice equally among six small (snack-size) self-sealing plastic bags. Place several chewy, fruit-flavored worms in each bag. Seal bag. Place bags in the freezer for several hours or until frozen. Remove ice from bags before using. Makes 6 ice pieces.

To make an ice ring, arrange chewy fruit worms in the bottom of a 4-cup ring. Pour juice into mold to almost cover worms. Do not allow the worms to float. Cover and place in freezer for 1 hour or until frozen.

spidery cookie wreaths

supplies

¾ cup butter
¾ cup sugar
¼ teaspoon baking powder
1 egg
1 teaspoon vanilla
1¾ cups flour
¼ cup finely chopped pecans or almonds
1 teaspoon grated orange peel
¼ teaspoon orange paste food coloring
1 recipe decorating icing
Decorating bag

continued on page 134

Writing tip #2
Red cinnamon candies or miniature candy-coated semisweet chocolate pieces, optional

what to do

1 In a large mixing bowl, beat the butter with an electric mixer on medium to high speed about 30 seconds or until softened. Add the sugar and baking powder. Beat until combined, scraping the sides of the bowl occasionally. Beat in the egg and vanilla. Beat in as much of the flour as you can with the mixer. Using a wooden spoon, stir in remaining flour.

2 Place half of the dough in a small mixing bowl. Stir in the pecans or almonds; set aside. To the remaining dough, knead in the orange peel and food coloring. Cover and chill both portions of dough about 30 minutes or until easy to handle.

3 On a lightly floured surface, shape each dough portion into a 12-inch-long log. Cut each log into twenty-four ½-inch-thick pieces. Roll each piece into a 6-inch-long rope. If necessary, cover and chill ropes for 10 to 15 minutes if soft and difficult to work with. Place a white and an orange rope side by side and twist together 5 or 6 times. Shape into a circle, gently pinching together the ends where they meet. Place on an ungreased cookie sheet. Repeat with remaining dough, leaving 2 inches between cookies. Bake in a 375° oven for 8 to 10 minutes or until edges are light brown. Cool on cookie sheet about 1 minute, then remove and cool thoroughly on a wire rack.

4 Using a decorating bag and writing tip #2, pipe icing into various-size spiders randomly on cookies. If desired, use red cinnamon candies, or candy-coated chocolate pieces for the body of the spider. Use a dab of icing to hold body on cookie. Let cookies stand until icing is set. Makes 24 cookies.

Decorating Icing: In a small mixing bowl, stir together 1 cup sifted powdered sugar and enough milk to make an icing of piping consistency. Tint with desired colors of paste or liquid food coloring. Makes ⅓ cup.

wrapped mummy sandwich loaf

supplies
- ¾ cup chopped green or red sweet pepper (1 medium)
- ½ cup chopped carrot
- 1 tablespoon butter or margarine
- 1 cup sliced fresh mushrooms
- 1 3-ounce package cream cheese or cream cheese with chives
- ½ of a 10-ounce package frozen chopped spinach, thawed and well drained
- 2 ounces thinly sliced Canadian-style bacon, cooked ham, or pepperoni, chopped (½ cup)

¼ **cup fine dry bread crumbs**
1 teaspoon dried Italian seasoning, crushed
1 16-ounce loaf frozen white bread dough, thawed
Milk
Sesame seeds or grated Parmesan cheese, optional

what to do

1 In a large skillet, cook and stir sweet pepper and carrot in hot butter or margarine for 2 minutes. Add mushrooms; cook and stir about 2 minutes more or until vegetables are tender. Remove from heat. Stir in cream cheese, spinach, meat, bread crumbs, and Italian seasoning.

2 On a lightly floured surface, roll dough into a 12×9-inch rectangle. Carefully transfer to a greased baking sheet. Spread the filling lengthwise in a 3-inch-wide strip down the center of rectangle to within 1 inch of the ends.

3 On both long sides, make 3-inch cuts from the edges toward the center at 1-inch intervals. Moisten the end of each dough strip. Starting at one end, alternately fold opposite strips of dough at an angle across filling. Slightly press moistened ends together in center to seal. Cover and let rise in a warm place until nearly double (about 30 minutes).

4 Lightly brush loaf with milk. If desired, sprinkle with sesame seeds or Parmesan cheese. Bake in a 350° oven for 25 to 30 minutes or until golden brown. Cool slightly on a wire rack. Using a serrated knife, cut into slices. Makes 12 slices.

sticks-and-stones snack mix

supplies

3 cups puffed corn cereal
2 cups crispy corn and rice cereal
2½ cups tiny pretzel sticks
1½ cups salted mixed nuts or shelled pumpkin seeds
3 tablespoons butter or margarine
1 tablespoon Worcestershire sauce
1 to 1½ teaspoons chili powder or barbecue spice
½ to ¾ teaspoon garlic powder
3 cups crunchy cheese-flavor snacks

what to do

1 In a 15×11×2-inch baking pan, combine the corn cereal, corn and rice cereal, pretzel sticks, and mixed nuts or pumpkin seeds.

2 In a small saucepan, heat butter or margarine, Worcestershire sauce, chili powder or barbecue spice, and garlic powder over low heat until butter melts. Drizzle over cereal mixture, tossing to coat.

3 Bake in a 300° oven for 30 minutes, stirring once or twice. Add cheese-flavored snacks, tossing to mix. Spread on foil; cool. Store in an airtight container for up to 5 days. Makes about 11 cups.

Celebrate Halloween by dressing the tabletop with clever screen place mats and cobweb-etched jars perfect for sweet treats or colorful beverages.

table trims

halloween place mat

supplies
Old place mat
Cloth window
  screen fabric
Scissors
Waxed paper
2 to 3 yards of
  $1\frac{1}{4}$-inch-wide
  ribbon
Thick white crafts
  glue
Narrow rickrack

what to do
1 Use an old place mat as a pattern to cut shape from screen.

2 Place window screen on a piece of waxed paper. Cut ribbon in lengths to fit each edge of mat, cutting corners at an angle for a mitered look. Apply glue to back side of each strip of ribbon and lay ribbon along each edge of window screen mat.

3 Turn window screen over and repeat the process for the back side.

4 On one side of the place mat, glue a continuous length of narrow rickrack to inside edge of ribbon.

eerie etched jar

supplies
Tracing paper
Pencil
Typing paper
Scissors
Pint-size jar with
  wide mouth
Vinegar
Black shiny paint
  pen
Crafts knife; cloth
Glass etching
  cream

what to do
1 Trace the pattern, *right,* and transfer design to strip of paper cut the height of the jar and long enough to wrap around the jar.

2 Wash jar in hot water with vinegar. Let dry.

3 Slip the paper pattern inside the jar with the pattern facing toward the outside of the jar.

4 Use black paint pen to trace the seven spokes of the web. Allow the paint to dry. When dry, add the connecting lines to the spokes of the web. Allow the paint to dry. Use a crafts knife to scrape away unwanted paint.

5 With a cloth dipped in vinegar, remove fingerprints from the sides of the jar.

6 Follow the directions on the jar of the etching cream to apply cream to the entire surface of the jar.

7 Wash away etching cream. Peel off paint pen. Let dry.

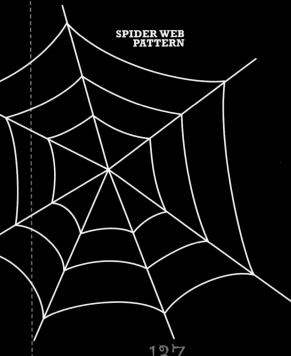

SPIDER WEB PATTERN

beanbag toss

Ready...aim...toss! Kids will love to play this party game, adding up points by tossing pumpkin-, ghost-, and cat-shape felt beanbags into the openings in the pumpkin. When not in use, place the pumpkin in the yard for all to see and enjoy.

supplies for pumpkin board

Pencil
4x4-foot ½-inch-thick exterior fir plywood
Jigsaw; sandpaper
Exterior paint in bright orange, dark orange, and black
1x4x30-inch fir (brace)
1½x2½-inch butt hinge with screws
16-inch light-duty chain with two ½-inch-long screws to fit
Drill and drill bit
24 inches of No. 9 wire (handle)

supplies for beanbags

(one of each shape)
Tracing paper
Pencil
**Two 5-inch squares
each of white
and orange felt**
**Two 6-inch squares
of black felt**
**Water-erasable
marking pen**
Scissors
**Small scrap of
green calico**
**Black and white
embroidery floss**
Needle
Beans or rice
Pinking shears

what to do

1 For the pumpkin board, enlarge the pumpkin pattern, *page 141,* and trace onto sheet of plywood. Cut out with saw. Cut out eyes, nose, and mouth. Sand the edges. Paint the entire pumpkin bright orange. Let dry. Paint the lines around the eyes black and the remaining lines dark orange.

2 Attach the brace to back at top edge using hinge. Screw chain between brace and pumpkin at bottom edge. Drill holes in top of pumpkin 1½ inches from top and 4 inches from sides. Attach wire through holes.

3 For beanbags, enlarge the patterns, *page 140,* onto tracing paper. Transfer each design onto one square of felt (ghost on white, pumpkin on orange, and cat on black) using marking pen. (Note: Do not cut out.) Cut a 1½x2¾-inch rectangle from green calico for the pumpkin stem.

4 Using all six plies of the embroidery floss, and referring to dots on patterns, work black French knots for ghost eyes, white French knots for cat eyes, and black Xs for pumpkin eyes. Work black backstitches for pumpkin smile.

5 For pumpkin stem, fold calico in half crosswise, right sides together, to form a ¾x1⅝-inch rectangle. Using ¼ inch seams, sew short sides. Turn right side out. Press under ¼ inch on raw edge.

6 Place the embroidered square atop unstitched square, wrong sides facing. Pin pumpkin stem to top of pumpkin as indicated by Xs on pattern. Stitch along sewing line, leaving opening as indicated by slashes on pattern. Fill bags with beans or rice, then sew openings closed. Cut out ¼ inch from seam using pinking shears.

continued on page 140

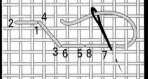

FRENCH KNOT (LEFT)

BACKSTITCH (BELOW)

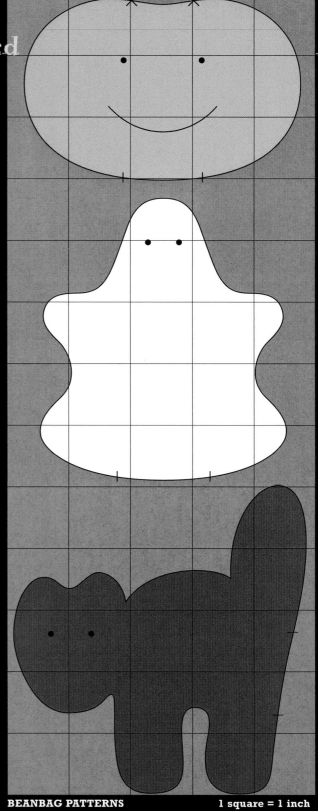

BEANBAG PATTERNS   1 square = 1 inch

PUMPKIN BOARD PATTERN

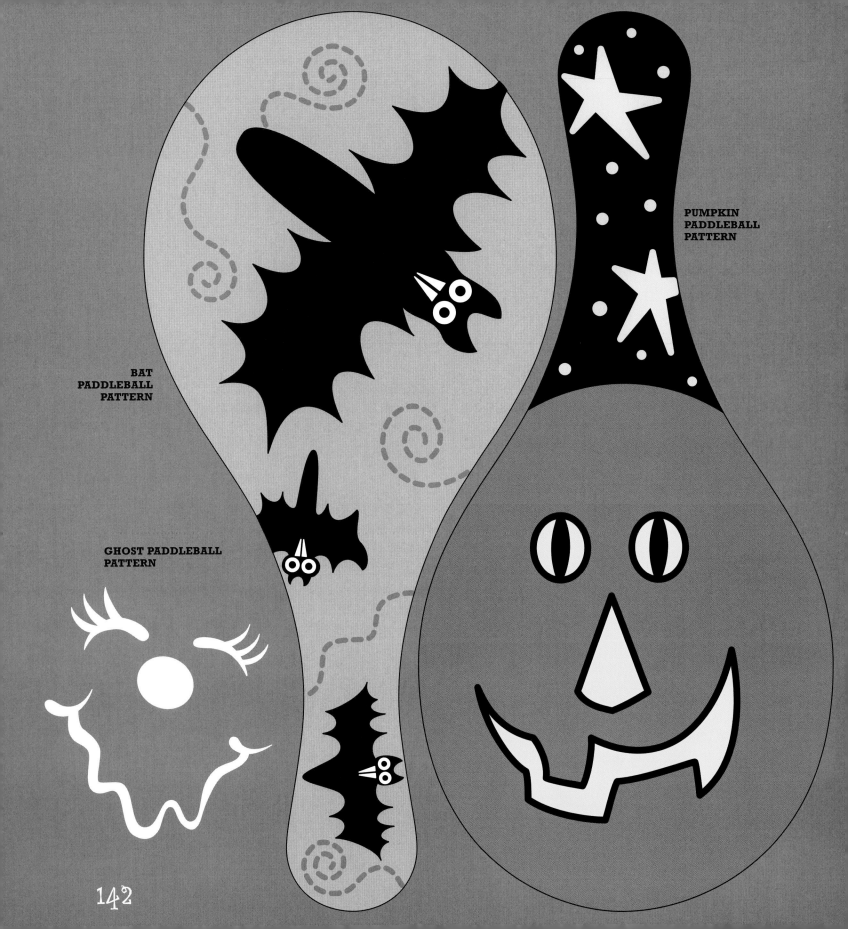

PUMPKIN
PADDLEBALL
PATTERN

BAT
PADDLEBALL
PATTERN

GHOST PADDLEBALL
PATTERN

142

playful paddleballs

Young guests will enjoy playing with (and taking home) these painted Halloween paddleball favors. Make them ahead using the patterns, opposite, or have the kids paint them at the party using their own Halloween designs. The paint dries quickly so the games will be ready to go when the guests start heading for home.

supplies
Acrylic paints in black, white, gray, orange, and yellow
Paintbrush
Purchased paddleballs
Tracing paper
Pencil with round-tip eraser
Transfer paper
Silver marking pen

what to do
1 Paint the background color of the design on the entire back of the paddle and sides. Paint the background for the ghost white, the pumpkin orange, and the bats gray. Let the paint dry.

2 Trace the desired patterns, *opposite.* Use transfer paper to transfer the details to the painted side of the paddleball. Paint in the details using the patterns as a guide. Let the paint dry. To make eyes on the bats, dip the eraser end of a pencil or the handle end of a paintbrush into white paint and dot onto the heads of the bats. Let the paint dry. Add smaller black dots in the center of each eye. Let the paint dry.

3 Use a silver marking pen to add dotted-line swirls to the bat paddleball board.

4 Paint the attached balls using the photograph, *right,* for inspiration. Let the paint dry.

143

Spooky

Disguises to scare them silly

masks

handheld masks,

see pages 152–159.

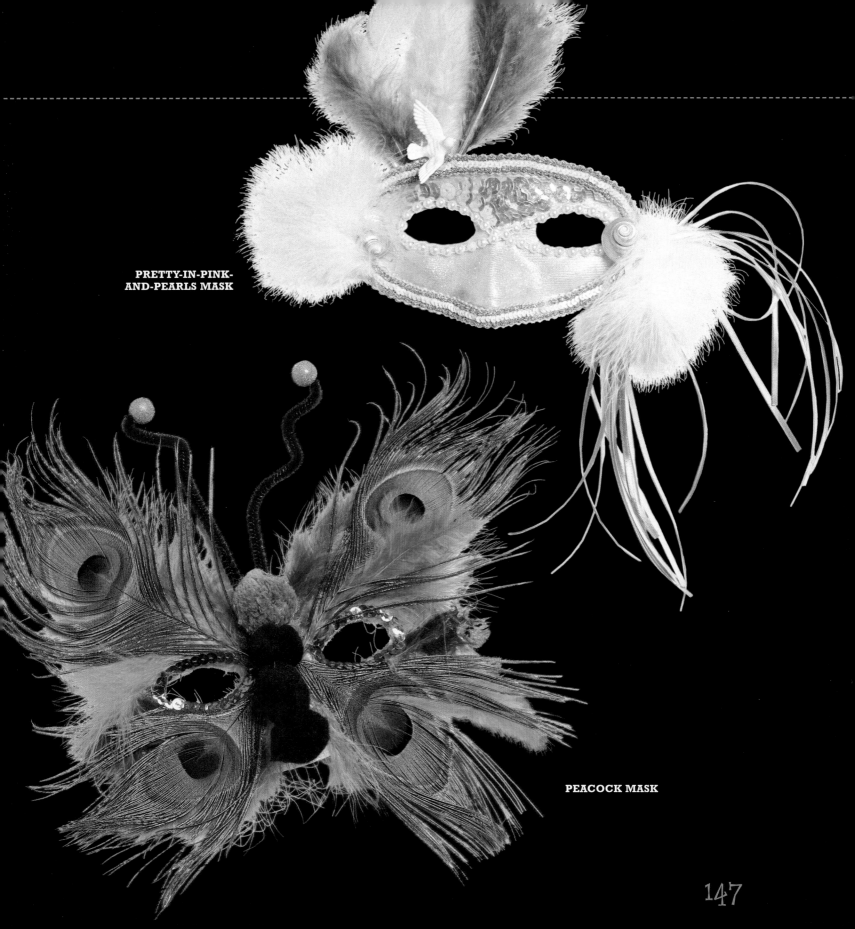

PRETTY-IN-PINK-AND-PEARLS MASK

PEACOCK MASK

147

pull-away masks continued

it's-a-hoot mask

supplies

Tracing paper
Pencil
Scissors
Heavyweight felt in cream, tan, dark brown, and black
Thick white crafts glue
Mask form that covers only eyes and nose
Hot-glue gun and hot-glue sticks
14-inch-long string of sequins for top piece and 24-inch-long string of sequins for beak and eyes
Single sequins
24-inch-length of ¼-inch dowel

what to do

1 Trace the patterns, *pages 150–151,* onto tracing paper. Cut out and trace onto felt. Cut out pieces.

2 Spread plenty of crafts glue onto the mask and glue the large dark brown piece on top. Place the point just above the nose area. The top will extend above the mask form.

3 Glue on all the tan felt feathers. Start from the top and work downward. Tuck the top feather under the dark brown felt. Tuck each feather under the previous one, gluing as you go. Lay down the four small feathers. Two large feathers should be on the bottom. The feathers should cover the side and down around to the nose area. They should not overlap into the eye area. They will hang well over the edges of the mask form. Do the remaining side the same way. Adjust each side so they look symmetrical.

4 Glue on black felt eyes. These should cover the ends of the feathers. Work from the inside of the mask and trim out eye holes with scissors.

5 Glue on the large cream-colored felt piece. The top edge should line up right along the top edge of the dark brown. Tuck the top edge of the black eyes under the cream felt.

6 Glue on the beak. Place the center top right below the dark brown felt point.

Fold the felt slightly to fit around the nose shape. Glue the edges down with thick white crafts glue or use a hot-glue gun.

7 Trim around beak, eyes, and top felt piece with strings of sequins. Glue in place using hot-glue. Glue sequins on the tips of feathers.

8 Glue the dowel between the edge and eyehole on inside of mask.

pretty-in-pink-and-pearls mask

supplies

White eye mask
Pink acrylic paint
Paintbrush
Decoupage medium
Iridescent white glitter
Hot-glue gun and hot-glue sticks
18-inch piece of pink braided trim

Thick white crafts glue
12-inch piece pearl bead trim
Iridescent sequins
Several feathers in pink, mauve, and white
Small plastic bird
Twelve 12-inch strands ribbon
2 balls feather fur
2 white iridescent shells

what to do

1 Paint mask soft pink color. Let the paint dry.

2 Paint on a thin coat of decoupage medium. Sprinkle on glitter. Let dry.

3 Use hot glue to attach braided trim around the outer edge.

4 Use crafts glue to glue on pearl bead trim around eye area, crossing over in the middle to make a figure eight.

5 Spread thick white crafts glue in area above eyes and fill in with iridescent sequins.

6 Using hot glue, attach pink, mauve, and white feathers to top of mask on the back side. Glue a small plastic bird to top of the mask.

7 Bundle ribbon strands and fold in center. Tie center with a ribbon and hot-glue to the side of the mask.

8 Glue feather fur to each side of mask with hot glue. Glue a shell to each side.

peacock mask

supplies

Eye mask form
Thick white crafts glue
12 feathers in green, turquoise, and deep blue
Scissors
4 peacock feathers
Hot-glue gun and hot-glue sticks
Black chenille stems
2 beads
10-inch piece of green sequin trim
1 green and 3 black pom-poms

what to do

1 Coat base of mask with crafts glue. Cover mask with green, turquoise, and deep blue feathers. Place them symmetrically onto the mask. Place narrow end of feathers in center and extend outward.

2 Cut two peacock feathers about 6 inches long and two to about 4 inches long. Arrange onto the mask to look like a butterfly. Use the long ones on top and short ones on bottom. Place the ends in the center of the nose area and glue in place with hot glue, gluing only in the nose areas, where glue will be covered in the next step.

3 Fold black chenille stem in half, curl ends, and attach beads. Glue with hot glue onto center top portion of mask.

4 Outline eye area with crafts glue and attach string of green sequins around eye openings.

5 Glue on one green and three black pom-poms to form the butterfly body. This will cover the ends of feathers and glue.

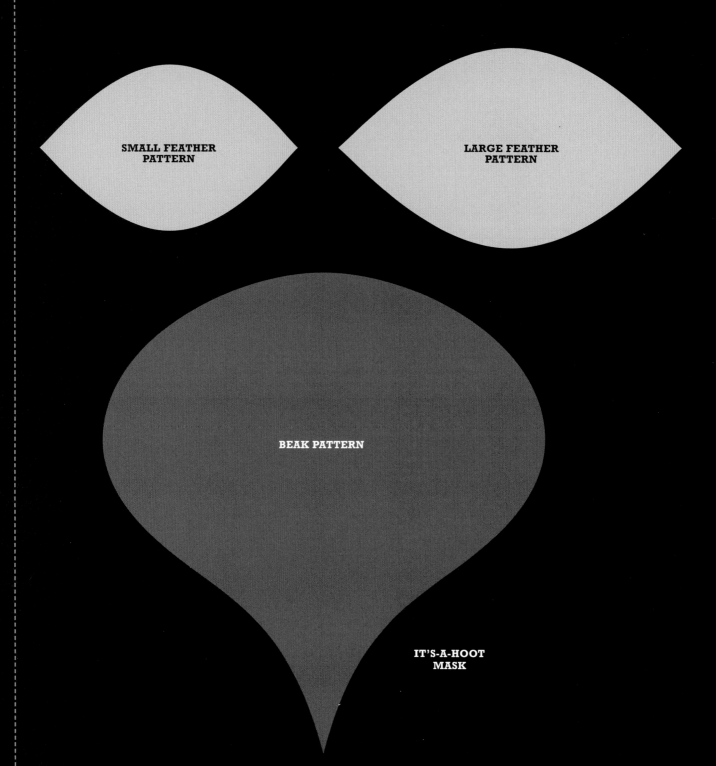

SMALL FEATHER
PATTERN

LARGE FEATHER
PATTERN

BEAK PATTERN

IT'S-A-HOOT
MASK

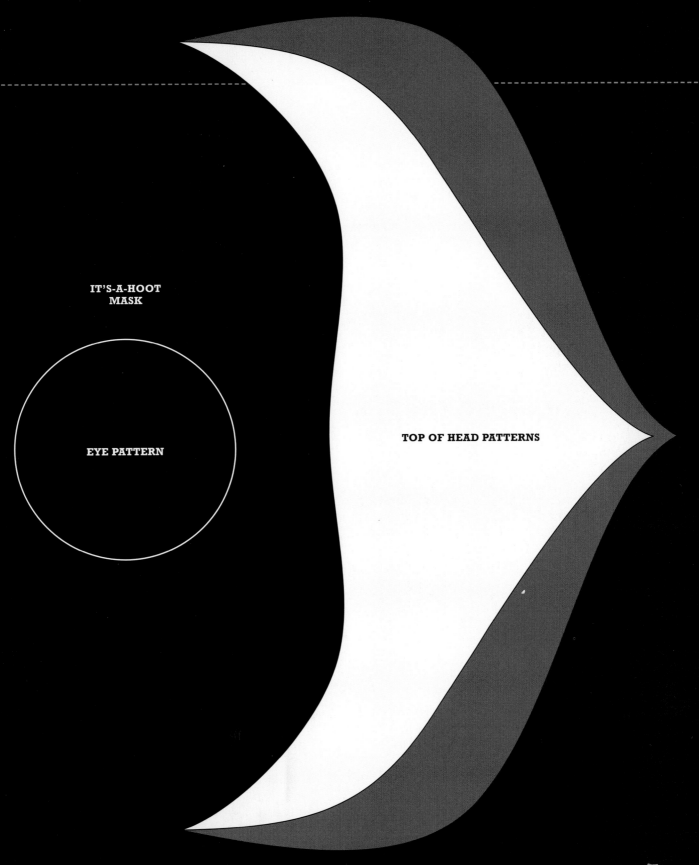

IT'S-A-HOOT
MASK

EYE PATTERN

TOP OF HEAD PATTERNS

151

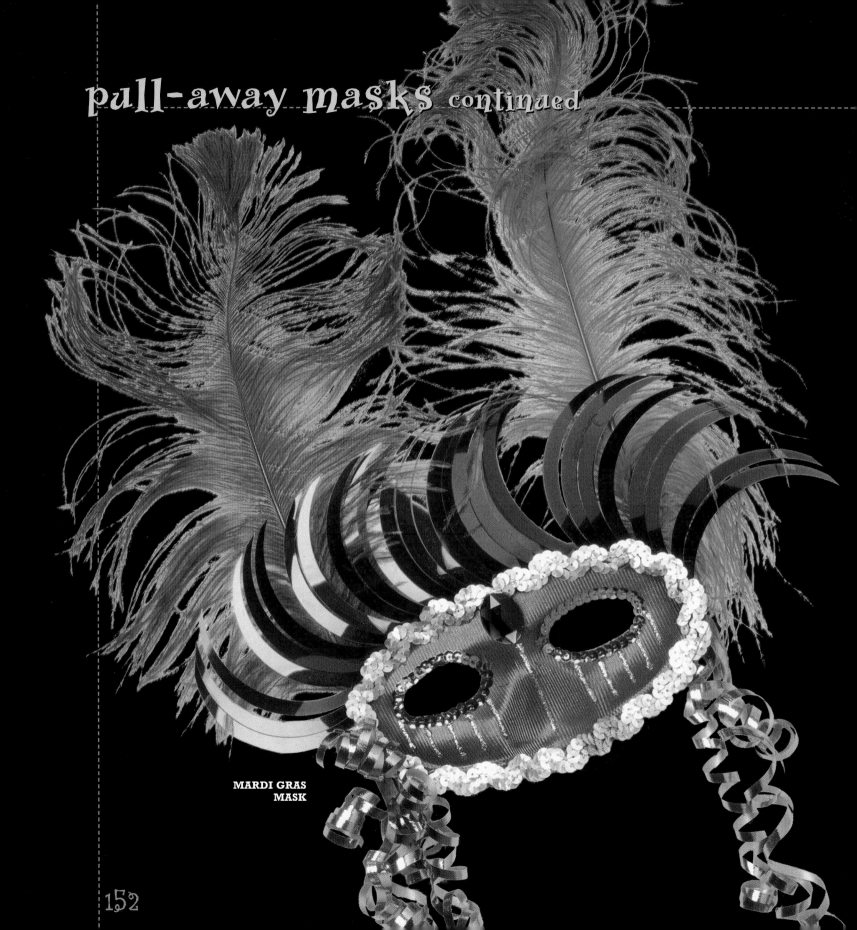

MARDI GRAS
MASK

**FRUITY
MASK**

**PHEASANT
FEATHER
MASK**

153

mardi gras mask

supplies

Purple mask or white mask painted with purple acrylic paint
8-inch piece of red metallic fringe
Hot-glue gun and hot-glue sticks
18-inch piece of gold sequin trim
Scissors
Thick white crafts glue
10-inch piece of green sequin trim
Green rhinestones
Glitter gold paint
Ostrich feathers in green and turquoise
60 inches of purple metallic curling ribbon

what to do

1 Use a purchased purple mask or paint a white one purple with acrylic paint. Let dry.

2 Glue the red metallic fringe to the top portion of mask with hot glue.

3 Hot-glue an 18-inch piece of gold sequin trim around edge. Trim off excess.

4 Outline eye opening with crafts glue. Attach green sequin trim around edge.

5 Hot-glue green rhinestones to center top.

6 Draw vertical lines down center and under eyes with glitter gold paint.

7 Hot-glue feathers to top back of mask.

8 Curl about 30 inches of purple metallic curling ribbon for each side of mask and glue to the sides.

fruity mask

supplies

White eye mask form
Yellow acrylic paint
Paintbrush
Tracing paper
Pencil
Scissors
Crafting foam in pink, red, and green
Hot-glue gun and hot-glue sticks
18-inch-long piece of purple sequin trim
Artificial flowers, fruit, and leaves
Glitter gold dimensional paint

what to do

1 Paint mask yellow. Let dry.

2 Trace curly shapes, *opposite,* onto tracing paper; cut out and trace onto pink and red foam. Cut out shapes. Glue onto front of mask alternating pink and red.

3 Glue on purple sequin trim around the edge of the mask.

4 For eyelashes, cut out small, thin triangles from green foam and glue in place.

5 Glue flowers, fruit, and leaves on the top and sides of the mask.

6 Trim the eyeholes with glitter gold dimensional paint.

pheasant feather mask

supplies
Paintbrush
Decoupage medium
Eye mask form
3 tablespoons of sand
Several pheasant feathers
Hot-glue gun and hot-glue stick
Preserved leaves or artificial leaves
Small pieces of evergreen
Shells
Gold glitter dimensional paint
Dried peas or corn
12-inch-long stick
Optional hanger

what to do

1 Paint a heavy coat of decoupage medium onto front surface of mask form. Sprinkle sand onto wet decoupage medium until covered. Shake off extra sand and let the decoupage medium dry.

2 Glue several pheasant feathers to one side of mask with hot-glue gun. Glue several smaller ones in center between eyes. Using glue gun, glue several fall-colored preserved or artificial leaves along the top and side.

3 Using hot glue, attach a small piece of evergreen and small shells over top of pheasant feathers on side.

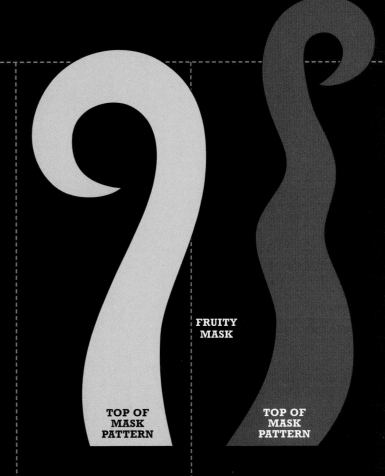

FRUITY MASK

TOP OF MASK PATTERN

TOP OF MASK PATTERN

4 Outline eye holes with glitter gold dimensional paint.

5 Outline outer edge of mask with glitter gold dimensional paint. Place small dried green peas or corn into gold paint and allow to dry.

6 Glue a stick to one side on the back.

7 Attach a hanger on the back side if you wish to hang the mask on the wall.

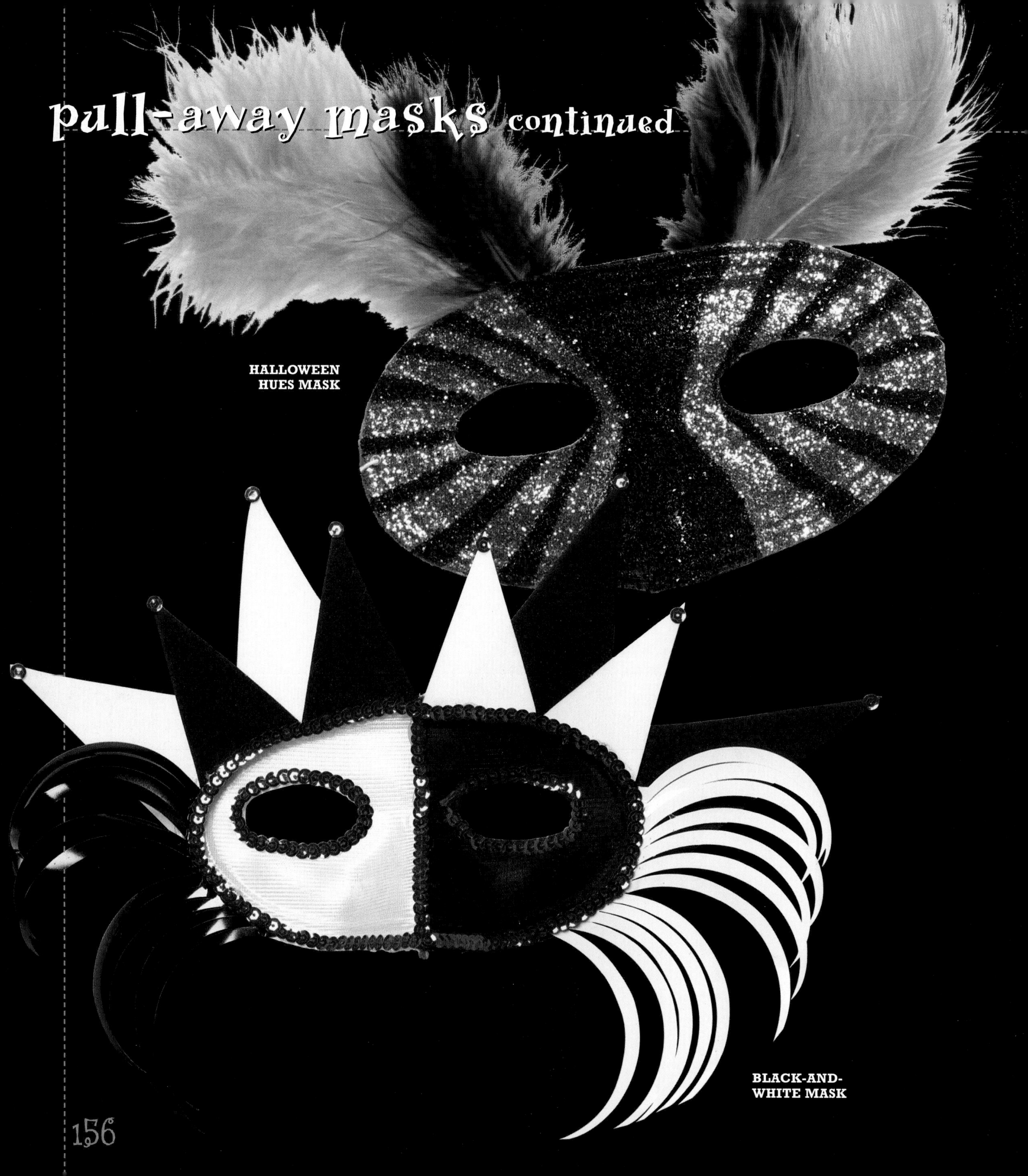

**HALLOWEEN
HUES MASK**

**BLACK-AND-
WHITE MASK**

JOLLY
JESTER
MASK

157

halloween hues mask

supplies
White eye mask form
Acrylic paints in orange and black
Paintbrush
Fine-pointed round paintbrush
Decoupage medium
Glitter in black and orange
Hot-glue gun and hot-glue stick
Feathers in black and orange

what to do
1 Paint entire mask orange. Let dry. Paint large black stripes down the center and thin black stripes from the eyes outward. Let dry.

2 Coat black paint with thick coat of decoupage medium. Paint on with brush. Sprinkle with black glitter.

Shake off excess glitter. Let the decoupage medium dry thoroughly.

3 Paint decoupage medium onto orange area. Sprinkle on orange glitter. Let dry.

4 Glue black and orange feathers to back of mask on each side. Let the glue dry.

black-and-white mask

supplies
White eye mask form
Black acrylic paint
Tracing paper
Pencil; scissors
Black and white fun foam
Hot-glue gun and hot-glue stick
Black and white ribbon fringed trim
Red sequined trim
Thick white crafts glue; sequins

what to do
1 Paint one half of white mask with black acrylic paint. Let dry

2 Trace patterns, *right,* onto tracing paper, cut out, trace onto fun foam and cut out. Cut two small black, two large black, two small white, two large white triangles. Hot glue along the top edge of mask. Glue white triangles above black half and black triangles above white half.

3 Glue black and white ribbon fringe trim to sides of mask. Glue black fringe onto white half and white fringe ribbon onto black half.

4 Glue red sequin trim around eyes, edge of mask, and down the center.

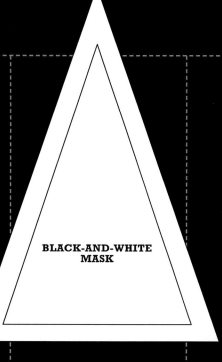

BLACK-AND-WHITE MASK

5 Glue sequins to the tip of each triangle.

jolly jester mask

supplies
Tracing paper
Pencil
Scissors
Self-adhesive coverings, such as Contact paper, in two colors
5 chenille stems
Gold glitter tube paint
5 jingle bells
2 purchased eye mask forms
Thick white crafts glue

²/₃ **yard of large rickrack**
Six 12-inch-long pieces of ¹/₄-inch-wide ribbon
24-inch-long stick

what to do

1 Trace triangle patterns, *right,* onto tracing paper and cut out. Use patterns to cut six large triangles from one color of Contact paper and four small triangles from the second color.

2 Remove the backing from two Contact triangles and center a chenille stem lengthwise between the two pieces. Lay the chenille stem ¹/₂ inch from the bottom edge and extend it beyond the top of the triangle. Firmly press the Contact paper pieces together. Repeat for the remaining triangles.

3 Outline both sides of each triangle with gold glitter paint.

4 Slip a bell on the chenille stem at the end of each triangle. Twist chenille stem to secure bell. Cut off the excess.

5 Cut the elastic off one of the masks. Glue two pieces of rickrack diagonally across the front of the mask. On the second mask, glue the three large triangles across the top of the mask. Overlapping the large triangles, glue the small triangles between the large ones.

6 Glue the first mask atop the second mask, sandwiching three

paper pieces together. Repeat for the remaining triangles.

lengths of ribbon on each side between the two masks. Place an end of the stick next to one group of ribbons to create a handle. Let the glue dry.

7 Glue rickrack across the top edge of the mask. Let the glue dry.

the-party's-here door mask

Set a distinct Halloween mood by greeting guests at the door with this creative work of art. An unusual combination of materials makes this decoration one that is bound to draw attention.

supplies

- 10x15-inch piece of cardboard
- 14x19-inch piece of purple metallic fabric or paper
- Tape; thick white crafts glue
- 9x14-inch piece of felt
- Small plastic mask form
- Copper-colored acrylic paint
- Paintbrush
- 50-inch-long string of gold sequins
- Wooden stars
- Green metallic acrylic paint
- Green glitter
- Sequins and rhinestones for corner stars
- ¾-inch-wide orange curling ribbon
- Ribbon shredder
- Scissors; pencil
- Gold trim to fit around mask
- 12-inch-long piece of green curling ribbon
- Rhinestones
- Hanger

what to do

1. Center the cardboard on top of the wrong side of the purple fabric or paper. Wrap the excess around cardboard and tape it to the back side.

2. Center and glue the felt piece to the back side of the covered cardboard.

3. Paint small plastic mask form with copper-colored acrylic paint. Paint two coats if necessary. Let dry.

4. Run a line of glue along the edge of the front of the purple board. Attach the string of gold sequins. Trim off the excess.

5. Paint the wooden stars with green metallic paint. Sprinkle green glitter if desired into wet paint. Let dry. Glue a star in each corner. Add sequins and rhinestones layered on top of each other onto each star.

6. Cut about eight 6-inch-long strips of ¾-inch-wide orange curling ribbon. Use a ribbon shredder to shred the ribbon except for about an inch on one end. Then using a pair of scissors, curl the shredded portion of ribbon in one sweep against the blade of scissors.

7. Place the mask onto the prepared purple board, centered, and trace around the edge. Remove the mask and glue curled orange ribbon pieces onto the mask area. Place each strand onto the purple surface in the top one-third portion of the head area. Glue the ends down inside the drawn pencil lines to be covered by the mask, allowing the curls to surround the top of the head.

8. Outline the remaining mask area with a generous amount of glue. Place mask down on top of ribbon and glue in place. Some glue should seep out along the edges.

9. Cut gold trim to fit around mask. Glue it down to cover glued edge of mask.

10. Curl a small amount of green curling ribbon and glue down on one side of head, Add rhinestones with glue.

11. Glue on a row of rhinestones along the eyebrow line. Add a hanger to the back of the board, centered near the top.

friendly lion mask

Tie on this adorable mask and you'll be off to see the wizard in no time. A heart-shape wreath forms the mane, leaving spaces for eyes and a mouth. For a wall hanging, glue plastic wiggly eyes over the eye holes.

supplies
Tracing paper
Pencil
Scissors
Felt in dark and light brown
Thick white crafts glue; stapler
Hot-glue gun and hot-glue sticks
Three 2-inch-thick wood hearts
Heart-shape twig wreath, approximately 8 inches across the inside center
Gold spray paint
Pair of black shoelaces

what to do

1 Trace ear patterns, *below,* and cut out. Use the large pattern to cut two pieces from light brown felt. Use the small pattern to cut two pieces from dark brown felt. Center and glue a small ear piece inside each large piece using crafts glue. Let the glue dry. Fold each ear in half vertically and staple near the fold at the bottom of each ear piece.

2 Use hot glue to attach the wood hearts as shown in the photograph. Add three hot-glue drops to each cheek. Let the glue dry.

3 In a well-ventilated area, cover the work surface. Spray-paint the wood heart cheeks/nose pieces. Let the paint dry.

4 Lay the wreath atop the dark brown felt. Trace the inside of the heart, approximately 1 inch from the inside edge of the wreath. Remove wreath and trim outside heart shape, 3 inches from the inside heart shape.

5 Use hot glue to attach the cheeks/nose piece to the top center point and sides of the wreath. Glue the ears to the top of the heart shape. Let the glue dry.

6 Tie a shoelace to each side of the wreath back. Glue the felt heart over the back side of the wreath. Let the glue dry.

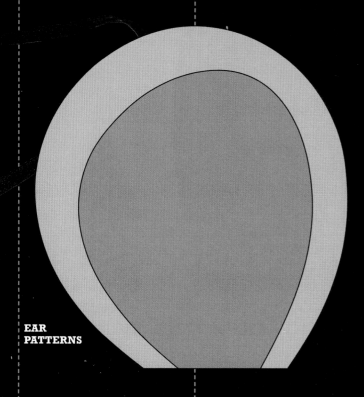

EAR PATTERNS

163

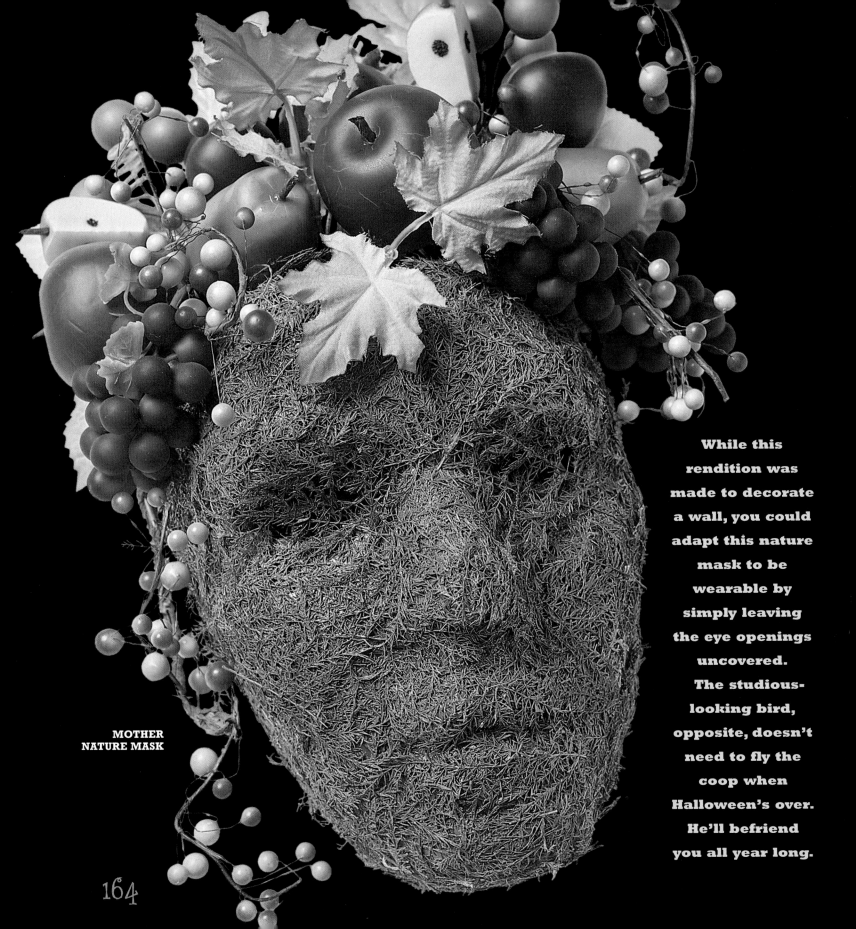

MOTHER
NATURE MASK

While this
rendition was
made to decorate
a wall, you could
adapt this nature
mask to be
wearable by
simply leaving
the eye openings
uncovered.
The studious-
looking bird,
opposite, doesn't
need to fly the
coop when
Halloween's over.
He'll befriend
you all year long.

wall wowers

mother nature mask

supplies
Plastic mask form
Foam core or cardboard; pencil
Sharp utility knife
Hot-glue gun and hot-glue sticks
5x7x2-inch plastic foam sheet, such as Styrofoam
5x3-inch piece of black felt; tape
Green acrylic paint
Paintbrush
Decoupage medium
Green fern, sphagnum moss, or preserved pliable leaves
Fall foliage and silk or plastic fruit; hanger

what to do
1 Trace outline of mask onto foam core or cardboard. Cut out shape with utility knife.

2 Using a hot-glue gun, glue a piece of plastic foam to the cutout cardboard to fit inside of mask.

3 Cut a piece of black felt approximately 5×3 inches and tape onto the foam block. Position it so it will show through the eye holes on the mask.

4 Tape the mask onto cutout board shape. Tape firmly around edges and onto back. Leave an opening on the top.

5 Paint the entire surface green. Paint a second coat if necessary. Let dry.

6 Paint a thick coat of decoupage medium on the green mask and press fern onto decoupage medium. Work a small section at a time. Continue adding fern pieces until the surface is well-covered. Coat with a final coat of decoupage medium. Let dry.

7 Insert an assortment of fall fruit pieces that come on picks into the foam block.

8 Add a hanger to the back.

bird of a different color

supplies
Newspapers
Plastic foam ball, such as Styrofoam, large enough to fill hole in lampshade top
Table knife
Square lampshade, approximately 12x12 inches
Thick white crafts glue
Waxed paper
Paper clay
Rolling pin

continued on page 166

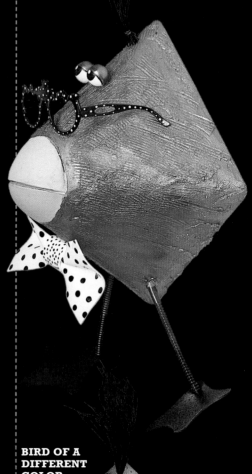

BIRD OF A DIFFERENT COLOR

STEP 1

STEP 2

STEP 3

STEP 4

STEP 5

STEP 6

Piece of string
Plaster of Paris
Plastic mixing tub
Spoon; old comb
Metallic acrylic
 paints in purple,
 blue, and teal,
 plus black,
 white, and gold
Paintbrush
Two 1-inch wooden
 doll heads
Child's sunglasses
 frames
Deep gray spray
 paint
Enamel paint in
 white and black
Purchased teal-
 colored feathers
Scissors
Pencil with
 round-tip eraser
Stapler
Tracing paper
White crafting
 foam
Crafts knife
Long flexible straw
Clear epoxy glue
8-inch piece of
 fine wire

what to do

1 Cover work surface with newspapers. Cut a foam ball in half using a table knife. Turn lampshade over and wedge foam into the top of lampshade. Add crafts glue around the edges of the foam to secure as shown in Step 1, *opposite*. Let dry.

2 Tear off two pieces of waxed paper. Sandwich a baseball-size piece of clay between the sheets. Use a rolling pin to flatten the clay to a thickness of about ¼ inch as shown in Step 2.

3 Remove clay piece and center it over foam ball in top of shade. Shape it to fit and trim excess with a knife as shown in Step 3.

4 While the clay is wet, pull a piece of string down onto the clay, shaping a mouth between two points of the shade as shown in Step 4. Let the clay dry.

5 Mix up 2 cups of plaster of Paris according to the manufacturer's instructions. Using a spoon, cover the outside of the shade, avoiding the clay beak as shown in Step 5. While wet, drag a comb over it to give a feather-like texture as shown in Step 6. Let dry.

6 Paint plaster areas using metallic acrylic paints as desired. Let dry. Paint the line across the beak black. Let dry. Paint the remainder of the beak gold. Let dry.

7 Paint doll heads white. Let dry. Paint dime-size black pupils. Let dry. Add a white dot to center of each eye. Let dry.

8 In a well-ventilated area, cover work surface with newspapers. Place glasses frames on newspapers. Spray-paint all sides gray. Let dry. Add white dots using enamel paint. Let dry.

9 Group a small tuft of feathers together. Wrap wire around ends. Trim feather ends straight.

10 Cut a 6×9- and a 2×5-inch piece from white foam. Paint large black dots on one side of large piece by dipping the eraser end of a pencil in paint and dotting on surface. Add small dots to one side of small foam piece using the handle end of a paintbrush. Let dry.

11 Accordion fold the large foam piece lengthwise. Wrap the small foam piece around the pleats. Staple.

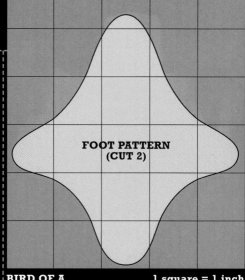

FOOT PATTERN
(CUT 2)

BIRD OF A DIFFERENT COLOR   1 square = 1 inch

12 Trace foot pattern, *above*, onto tracing paper. Cut out. Cut two from crafting foam. Cut a small X in the back of each foot piece using a crafts knife. Cut two 8-inch pieces from a straw. Paint the straws and foam feet using metallic paints. Let dry. Push one end of each straw through an X in the feet.

13 Use epoxy to glue the eyes, feathers, glasses, bow tie, and legs in place. Let dry. Add a wire hanger to the metal support of the lampshade.

index

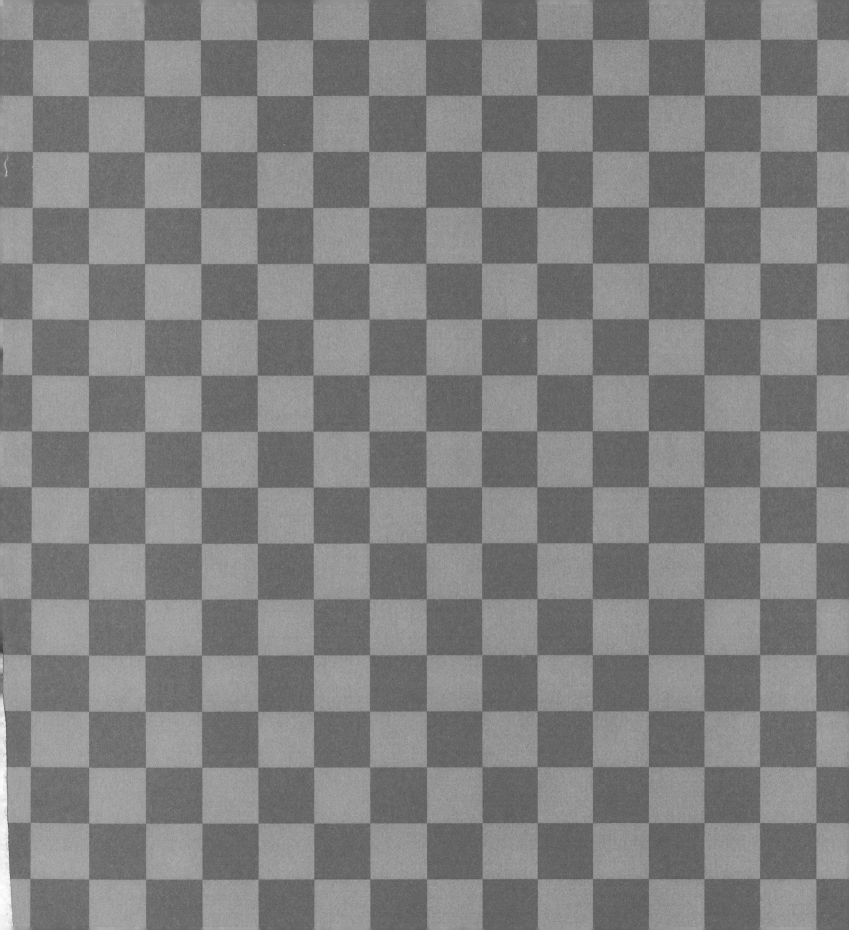